YOU ARE THE CELEBRITY

How to Become Famous

The Celebrity Guru DR.PPP

DR. PRAVIN P. PATEL.

Award Winning Author

You are the Celebrity
How to Become Famous

Youarethecelebritybook.com

Publisher
10-10-10 Publishing
Markham, ON
Canada

Printed in Canada and the United States of America

DEDICATION

To God, because everything is possible with God's blessings.

To my father Prahladbhai Patel, because he is also my godfather, as well as my #1 mentor, who taught me how dream and achieve it. You created me. I created this book. My creation of this book "You are the Celebrity" is going to make you proud.

To the love of my life Varsha, who brought me to North America and for giving me the most precious gift, our son Prem.

To my son Prem, my love.

To my late mom Dhuliben (Sitaben) Patel, for bringing me into this universe. I miss you a lot. I miss your love. Your loving memories are always with me.

To my second mom Surakshaben, for loving my father and giving a mother's love to me.

To my grandmother Joytiben, for living life at 90+ age strongly.

To my late grandfather, for your dedication for God.

To my mentors, which I mentioned in the first chapter.

To my relatives, for your love for me.

To my social media celebrity fans, for your unconditional love of my book for several years.

To Mittal Patel, Mina Baghaee,Kedisha Macknight, Kiri Varatharajan, Josephine RozenbergdeJongh for pre-ordering multiple copies internationally. Successful people like you see the opportunity and take action. You are action takers.

To you my reader, because you are the celebrity. My book is about realising that you are the celebrity.

To you, who picked up extra copy of this book for your loved one or recommended my book to your family, friends. relatives, colleagues, and strangers, as well as promoting on social media.

CONTENTS

TESTIMONIALS

Happy Birthday, Celebrity Guru, DR. PPP.

—MR. AMITABH BACHCHAN
BOLLYWOOD & HOLLYWOOD CELEBRITY

I paid to The Celebrity Guru, DR. PPP. (Not sure what he is saying here)

—MR. ANIL KAPOOR
BOLLYWOOD & HOLLYWOOD CELEBRITY

I know you, The Celebrity Guru, DR. PPP.

—DIA MIRZA
BOLLYWOOD CELEBRITY

The Celebrity Guru, DR. PPP, has not only followed me over 10 years in almost all my million dollars' seminars in CANADA but also in the USA, BAHAMAS, ST. MARTEEN, PUERTO RICO on land, above the sea, as well as on air too. I highly recommend you read his first baby, "You are the Celebrity".

"You are the Celebrity" helps you realize that you are the celebrity.

I endorse DR. PPP as your celebrity coach and celebrity speaker.

—RAYMOND AARON
NEY YORK TIMES BEST SELLING AUTHOR
RAYMONDAARON.COM

The Celebrity Guru, DR. PPP, is a very genuine and authentic person, who is interested in the success of his clients. He will take the time to help you achieve your celebrity status and the success that you truly deserve. The Celebrity Guru, DR. PPP, made me a celebrity and he will make you a celebrity, if you follow his wisdom in this book and by choosing his personal or group celebrity coaching, if you qualify. The Celebrity Guru, DR. PPP, is also and international celebrity speaker. I highly recommend him as a celebrity speaker in your country.

—AMIT AMBEGAONKAR
WEALTH AND BUSINESS COACH
YOURPROFOUNDSOLUTIONS.COM

ACKNOWLEDGEMENTS

I AM SPEECHLESS AND want to thank God for creating me with the purpose to make more than a dent in this universe. I don't have words to thank you, my father Prahladbhai Patel, for bringing me into this universe, being my godfather, as well as the world's #1 mentor. I thank you for raising me to be full of dreams. I am proud of you. The world is the best place to live, because of a father like you.

How can I express my acknowledgements towards my late mother Dhuliben (Sitaben), for keeping me in your body for about 9 months and bringing me into this universe to make more than a dent in it? I paid a huge price to get higher education by missing you.

Varsha, love of my life, you are the one who became the bridge between the east and the west and brought me all the way from India to North America in 1996.You gave me the most precious gift, our son Prem. I love you. I will keep loving you till my last breath.

Let me introduce another PPP, my son Perm Pravin Patel. You are the best son that any parents pray to God to have. I love you. I will keep loving you no matter what!

I am humbled to have my spiritual mentors, which I mentioned in chapter 1.

Oprah, Tony Robbins, and Bill Britt, how can I thank you? You are in my chapter 10. This world is the best place to live because of the legends like you.

I love Raymond Aaron, who has been in my life more than 10 years as my life mentor. Raymond, you are the celebrity guru maker. You are the guru of the gurus. You are the inspiration. May God keep blessing you in your mission. You are the author maker. You are the only person in the universe who wrote Chicken Soup for the Soul books & a Dummies book. Thank you for teaching life lessons on the land, above the ocean, as well as several thousand feet up in the air. This book was created because of you and the staff of Raymond Aaron Group, including Raymond's daughter Lauri, Liz, Wendy, Carla, Laura, Rosa, Naval, Chinmai, Vishal and more. I thank you for introducing the celebrities Jack Canfield, Bob Proctor, Dr. John Gray, Dr. Ivan Misner, JT Foxx, Laura Leighmier, Debra Poneman, Mark McKoy and more. Raymond, you made me speechless by arranging the best book launch party for me, by inviting Jack Canfield who has written over 250 books and sold 500 million copies in over 40 languages.

JT Foxx, you are really the #1 wealth coach. I love your influence in my life. Keep spreading your knowledge to eradicate poverty.

Jack Canfield, you made my book launch special and gave me your blessings for my huge success. You are one of the humblest people I've ever met in my life.

I thank you to the Get REAL with Raymond Group members, as well as the Raymond Aaron Retreats Group members for your unconditional love for me and my book "You are the Celebrity".

I thank you Ash Silva from Printing Icon, my editor as well as formator for their effort to have my book ready for you to transform your life.

I thank you my Facebook celebrity fans. You have seen the

cover of my book as well as my pictures and videos a million times. Finally, an end of your eagerness and wait. Its your time for action by ordering multiple copies all over the world and making my book "You are the Celebrity" an international best seller.

I am proud to announce that Mittal Patel, Kedeisha McKnight, Mina Baghaee.Kiri Varatharajan, Josephine RozenbergdeJongh have started the avalanche by pre-ordering multiple copies in multiple countries. You are the action takers.

I want to give an extreme thank you to my international accountability partners, Amit Ambegonkar, Glen Nielsen, and Laurie K. Grant.

To the Facebook & YouTube Queen Tanya Ortiz, I was speechless because of your hospitality during my inauguration tour for Mr. Trump. I've more surprises in chapter 5.

I thank you, because you are the celebrity.

FOREWORD

THE CELEBRITY GURU, DR. PPP, has not only followed me for over 10 years in almost all my million-dollar's worth of seminars in Canada, but also in USA, BAHAMAS, ST. MARTEEN, PUERTO RICO on the land, above the sea, as well as in air too. I personally coached DR.PPP in the business class of the plane. Generally, I charge over $5,000 USD per hour in the plane. DR.PPP and I took an MSC business cruise to the Caribbean, designed by Italian actress Sophia Lauren to teach deep life lessons away from home in total luxury.

I personally worked with DR. PPP during the days as well as the nights to deliver his first baby "You are the Celebrity" for you to make more than a dent in the universe. "You are the Celebrity" is a book that realizes you are the celebrity. I highly recommend ordering multiple copies to add value to the lives of your family, friends, and relatives, because sharing is caring, plus it's a donation of knowledge by giving books with the power to transform your life.

I highly endorse DR. PPP as the celebrity speaker, as well as the celebrity coach for you to fulfill your dreams. Let's make more than a dent in the universe by fulfilling The Celebrity Guru, DR.PPP'S vision to create a minimum of one million celebrities by the year 2025.

The Celebrity Guru, DR. PPP, met over one thousand celebrities from all over the world, e.g. spiritual celebrities, Bollywood celebrities, Hollywood celebrities, celebrity politicians, celebrity cricketers, famous tennis players, celebrity entrepreneurs, celebrity award winning authors and the list goes on and on.

The Celebrity Guru, DR. PPP, is the celebrity international adventurer who ran two marathons in one year in CANADA, went parasailing in BAHAMAS, bungee jumping and skydiving in NEW ZEALAND to inspire you by fulfilling his wildest dreams. Believe in your wildest dreams. Don't let anybody steal your dreams. If DR. PPP can do it, so can you.

—Raymond Aaron
New York Times Bestselling Author

ABOUT THE AUTHOR

THE CELEBRITY GURU, DR. PPP, is the soul that came from the supreme soul and is celebrating life as a celebrity author, a celebrity speaker, a celebrity coach, a celebrity doctor, a marathon man, a celebrity humanitarian, and a celebrity adventurer.

The Celebrity Guru, DR. PPP'S full name is DR. PRAVIN PRAHLADBHAI PATEL. DR. PPP born at the Temple Street, Jhulasan, India. The home of celebrity NASA astronaut Sunita Williams, as well as the famous Muslim Goddess Dolo MA temple. Jhulasan is in the Gujarat state of India. Gujarat gave the world lots of celebrities, including Mahatma Gandhi; two of India's Prime Ministers, Narendra Modi and Morarji Desai; as well as first deputy PM Sardar Patel, who combined 565 princely states to unite India.

The Celebrity Guru, DR. PPP, met over 10,000 celebrities from all over the world, e.g. spiritual celebrities, Bollywood celebrities, Hollywood celebrities, celebrity cricketers, celebrity Tennis Players, celebrity politicians, celebrity entrepreneurs, celebrity award winning authors and more, then collected their autographs, photographs, and interviewed them to share their secret to success with you through this book, "You are the Celebrity".

DR. PPP studied medicine in India and studied homeopathy in Canada. DR.PPP came to Canada in 1996, sponsored by love of his life, Varsha. DR.PPP has a son, Prem.

DR. PPP served in the Canadian army as a celebrity engineer to fulfill his childhood dream to become an engineer, as well as to serve the nation.

For DR. PPP'S rates and availability as The Celebrity Speaker, as well as The Celebrity Coach, please visit:

www.youaretheceelbirtybook.com, or
www.facebook.com/youarethecelebrity.

To order more books to be the part of the mission to make this book an international bestseller, please visit:

www.amazon.com or
www.youarethecelebritybook.com.

GENESIS

WELCOME TO THE award-winning author, The Celebrity Guru, DR. PPP's celebrity world. Are you ready to find real you? I congratulate you for taking time to start your success journey with the celebrity guru DR. PPP through your life changing book, "You are the Celebrity".

There were about 200 million to 500 million sperm ready to fertilize the ovum of your mom. Out of those 200 million to 500 million sperms, you came to the womb (uterus) of your own mom as the celebrity. Yes, you are the celebrity. You became one cell then multiplied. Now look at you, you are a powerhouse of multi-trillion cells. Yes, you are the celebrity. You were the soul with only one cell when you came to the womb of your mom. Now you are the soul with a powerhouse of multi trillion cells. Yes, you are the celebrity. How do you feel now to discover yourself? Excited, fired up, and on top of the world?

You are the celebrity who came to earth to celebrate your life and inspire the world. You are not the body of white, black, brown, yellow or any skin colour. You are not tall, short, thin, or fat. You are the soul. You are the soul that came from supreme soul to enlighten your soul and other souls on this planet.

The soul can't be cut by weapons. The soul can't burn by fire. The soul can not get wet by water. The soul can not dry by the wind. (The Gita 02-23) The Geeta is not only the holy book of The Hindus, but also humanity.

Let me share the genesis of award-winning author DR. Pravin P Patel (DR.PPP). About 25 years ago, my father Prahladbhai, who is not only my father but also my godfather, came to meet me at my medical hostel in Surat, India, from my birthplace Jhulasan, India. Surat is the diamond hub of the world. I was polished like a diamond in Surat by being surrounded with lots of celebrities from different fields. About 2,000 people out of the 5,000 people have migrated to North America. Jhulasan has the only Dolo Ma Temple in the world. Where the Muslim family was born, Dolo Ma is worshiped in the 100% Hindu population village JHULASAN. This is a huge example of world peace. Jhulasan is also the birthplace of NASA astronaut Sunita Williams' father. Sunita holds the records for total spacewalks by a woman (7) and the most spacewalk time for a woman (50 hours 40 min). Sunita also did a triathlon in the space. No wonder I am the award-winning marathon man. I was born in the temple street. No wonder I am full of spirituality.

I was so fired up to show my father my new adventure, that I started to write my autobiography. I told my father this news with an expectation of a great response. My father told me, "Son, why don't you become larger than life so that people will write your autobiography and other books about you." Wow! What an awesome life lesson! So, I stopped writing until I met my book mentor, as well as life mentor, Raymond Aaron who is a NEW YORKTIMES BESTSELLING AUTHOR.

I would like to share the genesis of I've experienced as unexplainable. unimaginable orgasmic moments by meeting almost 1,000 celebrities in the last 25+years., getting their autographs, photographs, and interviews in several countries. I met spiritual gurus, Bollywood celebrities, Hollywood celebrities, famous politicians, international Cricketers,

Tennis celebrities, celebrities in the positive mental attitude field, celebrity authors, celebrity entrepreneurs and more. I was pregnant with great inspirational thoughts by meeting those celebrities. I met one of my life mentors, RAYMONND AARON, who helped to deliver my beautiful baby for you, which I named "You are the Celebrity".

This book is about discovering the celebrity within you. I believe in you, even you don't believe in you. I believe in you, even if you don't believe in you and others don't believe in you. Basically, I believe in you because you are the celebrity. God never makes junk. You are the soul that came from supreme soul. You are unstoppable. You are beyond imagination. You are irresistible. You are the soul ready to awaken and inspire the universe.

I am excited to share in the first chapter the celebrities I have met. You must have seen some or lots of celebrities too. I would love to hear from you. How did you feel after meeting them? How eager were you to meet them? Did it increase your dream to meet bigger celebrities? Did I inspire you already?

I would love to hear from you and meet you. You never ever forget that you are the celebrity.

Visit www.youaretheceelbritybook.com to get your bonuses. You will discover that you are the celebrity by reading "You are the Celebrity" book. You become what you read. You were born as the celebrity. Live as the celebrity and your body will die, but you will be remembered as a celebrity.

CHAPTER 1

THE CELEBRITIES I MET

The purposes of this chapter are following:

1. I want to share one of the secrets to become the celebrity, UPBRANDING. One of the ways I up-brand myself is by associating with other celebrities. The celebrities always brand and up-brand. Out of sight means out of mind. I met almost 1,000 celebrities, got lots of autographs and photographs with them, as well as several hundred interviews with them in last 25+ years. I will keep associating till my last breath. The celebrities always brand and up-brand. In this world, you are either growing or dying, so get in motion and grow by having the right coach and learning the art of branding and up-branding. I am the celebrity coach. Feel free, if you are really serious, to have me as your celebrity coach by visiting youarethecelebritybook. com.

2. I want to make you realise that to be the celebrity you must surround yourself with other celebrities. The Law of Association teaches that you are who

you are because of the people you associate with. You are the average of your five closest friends. If you are not happy with your outcome, then start associating with the celebrities in the field where you want to become a celebrity and you will become a celebrity. If you are happy with where you are, then keep associating with those individuals.

3. I want you to know more about me so you feel that I am beside you during your reading of "You are the Celebrity" and after reading it, you put the principles of this book into practice in your life to become a celebrity.

4. To "WOW" you. More you say 'WOW' reading "You are the Celebrity", the more you feel connected with me. You will get more feel-good hormones. You will feel happier. The celebrity 'WOW' you will appear. That is one of the secrets to become a celebrity. My book mentor Raymond Aaron is the expert of BRANDING and UPBRANDING.

5. I want to inspire you to reach an inner circle of the celebrities. When you reach the inner circle of the celebrities, you will be really inspired. You write down a minimum of 10 celebrities in your field to become part of their inner circle. Make it your hobby to find out ways to reach the inner circle of those celebrities and put their success principles into practice in your life. Success is not complicated. Success is not the destination. Success is the journey. Enjoy the journey.

I felt unexplainable, unimaginable, orgasmic moments meeting almost a thousand celebrities in last 25+ years.

The Spiritual Celebrities I Met

Pramukh Swami
Pandurang Shastri Athvale
Dalai Lama
Asharam Bapu
Morari Bapu
Lalji Maharaj
Baba Ramdev
Tejendra Prasad
Swami Sachidanand
Sadhvi Rutambara
Avichal Das
Niruma
Dadi Prakashmani

The Celebrity Politicians I Met

Narendra Modi, India's PM
Bill Clinton, President of USA
Donald Trump, President of USA
Late DR.APJ Abdul Kalam MR. President of India
Late Rajiv Gandhi, India's PM
P V Narsimha Rao India's PM
Stephen Harper, Canada's PM
Dalton McGuinty
Kathleen Wynne
Shashi Tharur
Chimanbhai Patel
Narhari Amin
Yogendra Makwana
Mel Lastman
David Miller

Bob Buckhorn
& more

The Celebrity Cricketers I Met

Sachin Tendulkar
Madan Lal
Ashok Malhotra
Maninder Singh
Sanjay Manjrekar
Praveen Amre
Ramakant Acharekar
Kiran More
Duleep Mandis
Arjuna Ranatunga
Rohan Sunil Gawaskar
Wasim Akram
Narendra Hirwarni
Venkatesh Prasad
Bret Lee
Ian Bishop
Phil Simmons
Ajay Jadeja
Sanath Jayasuriya
Brendon McCullum
Tim Southee
Wasim Akram
Abdul Qadir
Aqib Javed
Aamir Sohail
Muddasar Nazar
Shoaib Malik
Shoaib Akhtar

Shahid Afridi
Hiral Patel
Rizwan Cheema
Atul Vasan
Harvindar Singh
Hemang Badani
Mohisn Kamal
Sunil Joshi
Sandeep Patil
Nayan Mongia
Robin Singh
Amit Bhandari
Shoaib Muhammad
Ijaz Ahmed
Naveed Anjum
Rashid Latif
Tauseef Ahmad
Manzoor Elahi
Mohisn Kamal
& more

The Tennis Celebrities I Met

Pete Sampras
Andre Agassi
Jim Courier
Roger Federer
Andy Roddick
Sarina Williams
Martina Hingis
Monica Seles
Mary Pierce
Milos Raonic

Sania Mirza
Mary Pearce
Caroline Wozniacki
& more

The Celebrities of Other Sports I Met

Milkha Singh
Mark McKoy
Sunita Williams
Michael "Pinball" Clemons
Rosie MacLennan
Karen Cockburn
Jason Burnett
& more

The Bollywood Celebrities I Met

Amitabh Bachchan
Shahrukh Khan
Salman Khan
Aamir Khan
Saif Ali Khan
Hritik Roshan
Dharmendra
Hema Malini
Sunny Deol
Bobby Deol
Esha Deol
Madhuri Dixit
Sridevi
Deepika Padukone
Dia Mirza, whose testimonial is on the back cover

Sharmila Tagore
Zeenat Aman
Preity Zinta
Rani Mukherjee
Amisha Patel
Javed Akhtar
Shabana Azmi
Farhan Akhtar
Govinda
Anil Kapoor
Rishi Kapoor
Rajiv Kapoor
Kareena Kapoor
Shahid Kapoor
Bonny Kapoor
Sanjay Kapoor
Sridevi
Priyanka Chopra
Prem Chopra
Sohail Khan
Arbaaz Khan
Malaika Arora
Nitin Mukesh
Akshay Kumar
John Abraham
A.R. Rahman
Hariharan
Ranveer Singh
Anuska Sharma
Kajol
Mallika Sherawat
Bipasha Basu
Boman Irani

Tusshar Kapoor
Arshad Warsi
Zayed Khan
Ashish Chaudhary
Omni Vaidya
Ritesh Deshmukh
Genelia D'Souza
Sonu Nigam
Adnan Sami
Manisha Koirala
Shilpa Shetty
Sunil Shetty
Shatrughan Sinha
Sonakshi Sinha
Juhi Chawla
Kangana Ranaut
Sonu Sood
Paresh Rawal
Anupam Kher
Nasseruddin Shah
Ratna Pathak
Om Puri
Dhanush
Sushmita Sen
Ramesh Sippy
Subhash Ghai
Karan Johar
Yash Johar
Rakeysh Omprakash Mehra
David Dhavan
Sajid Nadiyadwala
Mukesh Bhatt
Deepa Mehta

Omung Kumar
Gulshan Grover
Asha Bhosle
Sudesh Bhosle
Neha Dhupia
Rageshwari
Kavita Paudwal
Monali Thakur
Sonali Vajpayee
Mandakini
Shankar Mahadevan
Ehsaan Noorani
Loy Mandos
Rahat Fateh Ali Khan
Salim Sulaiman
Sajid
Vajid
Laxmikant
Pyarelal
Viju Shah
Raghav
Mahesh Kanoida
Naresh Kanodia
Asrani
Johnny Lever
Javed Jaffrey
Kapil Sharma
Raju Srivastav
Sugandha Mishra
Rohini Hattangadi
Viju Shah
Laxmikant
Pyarelal

Anu Malik
Arjun Rampal
Aditya Roy Kapoor
Divya Datta
Prasoon Joshi
Mithoon
Neeti Muhan
Javed Ali
Shweta Pandit
Benny Dayal
Arijit Singh
Shreya Ghoshal
Lisa Ray
Gulshan Grover
Kabir Bedi
Bali Brahmbhatt
Sujata Mehta
Leena Chandawarkar
Siddharth Randeria
Mahavir Shah
Ajit Vachani
Arvind Rathod
Firoz Irani
Raveena Tandon
Daler Mehndi
Mika Singh
Twinkal Khanna
Namarata Shirodkar
Ravi Bahal
Vijay Arora
Nalin Dave
Jashpal Bhatti
Altaf Raja

Rajendra Nath
Birbal
Sudhir
Varsha Usgaonkar
Raj Babbar
Neha Dhupia
Suman
Archana Puran Singh
Jr. Amitabh
Jr. Dev Anand
Jr. Madhuri
Jr. Sunny Deol
Jr. Anil Kapoor
Sarita Joshi
Rita Bhaduri
Rashik Dave
Salma Agha
Dhanush
Rati Agnihotri
Suman Ranganathan
Jaya Prada
Sonali Bendra
Prachi Desai
Harman Baweja
Ronit Roy
Aarti Chaabaria
Rahul Khanna
Kishan Kumar
Gauhar Khan
Richa Chadda
Aditi Rao Hydari
Kainat Arora
Vikas Bhalla

Samira Reddy
& more

The Hollywood Celebrities I Met

Oprah Winfrey
George Clooney
Hillary Swank
Al Pacino
John Travolta
Kevin Spacey
Robert Downey, Jr.
Cuba Gooding, Jr.
NSYNC Group
Ryan Gosling
Freida Pinto
& more

The Celebrity Entrepreneurs

Allan Kippax
J. Lloyd "Coach" Tomer
Bill Britt
Peggy Britt
Kanti Gala
Lata Gala
Kumar Shiva Ramakrishnan
Sugeet Ajmani
Kajal Ajmani
Velauther Arunasalam
Thilaka Arunasalam
Anjalee Kumar
Raj Shah

Sangita Shah
Manipal Reddy
Renuka Reddy
Paul Miller
Leslie Miller
Angelo Nardoni
Claudia Nardoni
Velauther Arunasalam
Thilaka Arunasalam
Tirthankar Dutta(TD)
Suparna Dutta
Nitin Soni
Parul Soni
Rocky Covinton
Phil Davies
Patrecia Davies
Murali Murthy
Shalul Kapoor
Jitu Alam
Reema Alam
Niran
Verni
& more

The Celebrity Authors

Raymond Aaron
Raymond Aaron's Celebrity Authors
Tony (Anthony) Robbins
Jack Canfield
Bob Proctor
Dr John Demartini
Deepak Chopra

Ashok Dave
Pitima Tongme
Murali Murthy
Raymond Young
Dan Blackburn
David Bach
Nicholas Boothman
Ken Dunn
Duke Johnson
& more

CHAPTER 2

MY MENTORS

THE MENTOR MAY be older or younger, but they have a certain area of expertise that you want to tap. It's a learning and development partnership between yourself and someone with vast experience. A life without a mentor is a life without direction. You need the right mentor to achieve your best life possible. Mentoring and coaching are not the same thing. Coaching is task oriented, short term and performance driven.

Mentoring is relationship oriented, always long term and performance driven. Basically, mentoring has a deeper meaning than coaching. Successful people have coaches as well as mentors. Every professional team has a coach. Almost every celebrity has coaches and mentors. You need coaches and mentors no matter what, if you want to be successful. Lord Krishna was the mentor for pandawa in the Mahabharata and through him the Geeta, the holy book of the Hindu, has arrived.

I am sharing the mentors I've got in my precious life, who have changed my life. I can not imagine life without them. Take your time to find your mentors. Once you find them, follow them to change your life. When you've got enough wisdom from your mentors, you become a mentor for others. The show must go on. I am honoured, humbled and privileged to share my first mentor with you.

My Father

Shri Prahladbhai is my father. My father taught me lots of life lessons. He is the visionary. He inspired lots of people and keep inspiring them. He has a vast knowledge of spirituality. He delivers motivational speeches. He loves to lead, especially by his example. One day, he brought my two brothers, Maheshbhai and Prakashbhai, and me to one of our three farms. We worked hard the whole day and, at the end of the day, he taught us the life lesson about importance of education. Education is important in life, helping us to appreciate how tough is physical work and without education, this would be what we are limited to. He always raises the bar for me to grow personally, educationally, and spiritually. He leads us like the authority that he truly is. His good reputation has spread through our village, district and the whole Gujarat province. I have witnessed lots of fathers come to my father for advice regarding their kid's educational future, marriage proposals and more. He always challenges himself and others. One of his mottos was to always make your friends smarter than you. He always read great books. Who you become is based on the people you associate and books you read. Your personal, financial, and spiritual growth is the average of your five closest friends. He always exercises and got us involved in plenty of physical activities. I learned to do a headstand during my childhood because of my father. Thanks to him, I never needed any stimulants, such as coffee, tea, or tobacco. Yes, I drank alcohol for a couple of months, but one day, I got drunk and the next day, I quit. I feel that God gave me so much energy, that I do not need any stimulants. I also believe you have the same supreme soul's energy, so you can also quit using external stimulants, such as coffee, tea, tobacco, alcohol, drugs or any of the other ones out there. I heartily urge you to quit tobacco, alcohol, and drugs for you and your loved ones' peace of mind. During my time in medical school, my father's support helped me survive. Every month or every other month, my father took time from his busy schedule to come and meet with me. He always wrote very inspirational letters to me and still I have those valuable letters with me. One day, that still I remember, just before my medical exams, I called and he was with me within the same day. During a plague, he specially hired a vehicle and came to my college to take me home. During my final year of medical college, he came to my school and solved a critical issue. For detailed information, you have to wait till my autobiography comes out.

In January 1994, my father asked me for first time if I was in love and if I was, to feel free to tell him so. I told my father that if I was in love, I would have told you. My father then told me that there was a family who wants you as their son-in-law. You can have a look and decide. On January 6, 1994, I saw for the first time Varsha and her relatives and I her and her amazing family. On February 5, 1994, I got married with Varsha, who was living in Canada. For more details, you have to wait for my autobiography. I came to Canada in July 23, 1996. Destiny brought me from the East to the West. You can put DR. PPP anywhere in the world, but you cannot take INDIA out of DR. PPP. I could write several books about the greatness of my father and still never be able to express all my feelings about my father. Papa is the word I have used to talk to my father all my life. Dear papa, thank you for bringing me into this universe. I was, I am & I will always love you, no matter what!

Now I am eager to introduce my spiritual mentors to you. I always put God first. All the glory goes to God. Somebody said that if I find God through my spiritual guru, then I will pay respect to my spiritual guru first, then God. This is because without the spiritual guru, I would not be able to find God. Without further delay, here comes my spiritual gurus for you.

Spiritual Gurus (Mentors)

Spiritual mentors are needed in life too. You go to a medical college to become a doctor. You go to an engineering college to become an engineer. You need a spiritual mentor to realise the spirituality of your soul and to have peace of mind and spirit. Its not only if you want to be a priest that you need a spiritual mentor (Guru).

When I was a kid, Lalji Maharaj, one of the spiritual leaders (Guru) came to my home, and he spoke the holy words in my ear and still I remember that incidence with crystal clarity.

PANDURANG ATHAVALE (DADA)

When I was in my early teens, my father started following Pandurang Athavale. Once a week, he used to lead my villagers in learning one of Pandurang Athavale's teachings called the SWAYDHYAY, the bridge between soul and supreme soul. One day, my father and I went to see him. I learned a lot from his spiritual teaching. In 2003, I went to see him in New York. I want to share that incidence with you. I informed my uncle that I would be coming down from Toronto to New York to meet Pandurang Athavale. After meeting him, I planned to meet up with him and his family. I went to New York from Toronto by bus. About noon, I went to his store and met my cousin. I told him I would be coming to your home tonight. I went to meet Pandurang Asheville and his devotees at a huge area in New York. I saw him in person with his devotees, a crowd of about

25,000, who came all over the world. I knew that this was the last chance I had to meet him and it really happened that way. The next time, I saw his ashes and I was heart broken. But that night after the program, I called my uncle to go to his home. He asked me why I had come to New York and I explained why and reminded him of the conversation we had before I left Toronto. I sensed that my uncle did not seem happy to bring me into his home. My heart was broken. So, I went to a hotel and asked what it cost for a night's stay. I don't remember the exact amount, but I know it was more than my budget. I started walking back toward the venue and then a miracle happened. A lady, who had attended the same function, approached me and offered me a place to stay for the night. This is power of the right association. God sent that lady to rescue me. The next day, I went to my aunt's home in New Jersey. This experience will give you giant lesson about God's miracles and angels. Pandurang Athavale's daughter Jayshree Talwalkar (DIDI), who is now the next big leader of swaydhyay parivar, brought his ashes to Toronto and I went there to pay my final respects to my spiritual leader.

HH. ASARAM BAPU

Asumal Sirumalani, as he is known by his followers, is the Hindu religious leader from India born on 17 April, 1941. During my early life in Surat, India, while I was studying medicine, I saw Asaram Bapu and lots of devotees having a huge celebration. I was amazed by Asaram Bapu's aura. I was attracted to him like a magnet. My body, mind and soul were full of joy and happiness. Asaram Bapu was in a pure white outfit that formed to his huge, tall, fit body, and a long beard. One of the most handsome personalities I had ever met. I came to learn that Asharam Bapu has ashrams all over INDIA, including Surat.

I started to attend when he was in SURAT. I made him one of my gurus and took diksha, which means a "preparation or concentration for a religious ceremony, giving of a mantra or an invitation by the guru in Indian religion, such as Hinduism, Buddhism and Jainism". I was on cloud 9. I also got to attend Holi celebration at SURAT'S ashram. I felt the LORD KRISHNA (one of the Hindu Messengers) in him. I was delighted to get colored personally by him. He was on a huge truck and through a pipe, he was showering all the devotees with color. I felt like LORD KRISHNA was doing leela. It was a powerful spiritual experience for me.

One day, I was attending his shibir. I did not have enough money and I had to stay there overnight. One of the soldiers taking care of the security of the ashram allowed me in his camp overnight. One night, I was sleeping overnight at the ashram while attending the shibir (yoga seminar). It was about 11 pm, and most of the participants were sleeping. I was awake and standing, observing all those staying at the ashram. I saw Asaram Bapu raise his voice as he talked to one participant who was suffering from TB (Tuberculosis) about health. As soon as Asaram Bapu saw me, Bapu said SO JA, which means go to sleep. That blessing from Bapu I took it as his Prasad to be calm in life.

Thousands of devotees listen to him with peace of mind and calmness. His ashrams are such peaceful places. Lots of holy books are available about Hinduism and Asaram Bapu, as well as pictures, Cassets, and remedies that were sold there for affordable price.

On another occasion, Bapu was at Ahmedabad Ashram, which is about 40 kms from my village JHULASAN.

I attended shibir there. I felt peace of mind. I loved meditating there.

I have to let you know that a couple of years ago, Asaram

Bapu and his son, Narayan, were put in to jail because of an allegation of rape. Let the truth prevail.

HH. Pramukh Swami (BAPA)

During my days at the medical college, my hostel room partner, Dr. Kirti Patel, brought me to HH Pramukh Swami when he was doing a morning walk at the private bungalow. I saw him for the first time for about 30 minutes from just a few feet away. I felt an incredible peace of mind. He was so calm.

I also had chance to see him performing a morning prayer at Surat BAPS Temple in front of thousands of devotees.

One day, I was sitting on the back seat of my uncle's scooter. He stopped at a gas station. I was stressed about my upcoming medical exam. I saw Pramukh Swami's picture by the pole of the gas station where my uncle had stopped his scooter. I looked at his picture and felt that same peace of mind.

I also visited the BAPS Toronto temple a few times, but that changed after one of my relatives had a life altering experience.

I've witnessed my father in law Mr. Kantilla Patel's life change by accepting BAPS. I promised myself that I would visit the temple frequently, at least once a week minimum, from that moment onwards. I started to visit that temple frequently. I asked some spiritual questions to the priests at BAPS Temple in Toronto. I became BAPS devotee on December 27, 2015. I am not claiming that I follow every event, although I would like to. When I saw Pramukh Swami through video streams, I almost always cried because even though he was 94, he was still spreading a message of God, Love, Respect, Humanity, Prayer and more. India's President DR. A.P. J. ABDUL KALAM with ARUN TIWARI wrote the book "TRANSCENDENCE: My Spiritual Experiences with PRAMUKH SWAMIJI". I was privileged to meet DR. A.P.J. ABDUL KALAM. I rarely see the fusion of two celebrities with different religious backgrounds, yet both were spreading the message of HUMANITY, LOVE and PEACE.

Pramukh Swami's guidance has led to over 1,000 temples being created all over the world. His teaching and guidance also inspired more than 1,000 young students to become priests all over the world. I visited the largest Hindu temple in the world in New Jersey (BAPS.ORG) on AUG 11 & 12, 2016 and it was being built under Pramukh Swami's blessings.

On August 13,2016, I woke up my brother Prakashbhai's home in South Carolina to the news that Pramukh Swami had left the world with millions of devotees globally. Within the next several days, the next BAPS guru HH. MAHANT SWAMI was appointed by will of Pramukh Swami. He is my next spiritual guru. I am super excited because HH Mahant Swami has scheduled his first visit abroad after being named the main guru of BAPS, and it will be in Toronto where I have lived almost half of my life. He will be there to celebrate the 10th anniversary of the BAPS Temple, Toronto, from July 19-27, 2017.

My spiritual mentors gave me lots of spiritual powers. They became the bridge between GOD, THE SUPREME SOUL and my SOUL. I've learned many lessons of love, peace, humanity and more. I up-branded myself by associating with them.

You need spiritual gurus in your life. If you don't have one, find the right one and allow him toshine in your life by learning life lessons from him.

I also highly recommend you read The Geeta, which is the Holy Book of Hinduism; The Bible for Christianity; and The Quran for Islam, plus other holy books of other religions.

I can share more about the divine experiences I've had because of the spiritual gurus in my life, but no matter how much I express; I will never be able to give justice to it.

I am extremely excited to share my other live mentors with you. Are you extremely excited too? I hear you. I feel you.

RAYMOND AARON

Raymond is my life mentor. A New York Times bestselling author, Raymond is the celebrity maker coach, awarding author maker, the real estate guru, the adventurer, and the connector. He owns over 40 businesses. Not only is he my book mentor, he is my book publishertoo. He is one of the reasons you are holding my book "You are the Celebrity". Throughout his writing career, he wrote 9 books. He wrote not one, but two chicken soup series books (Chicken Soup for the Canadian soul and Chicken Soup for Parent Soul). He also wrote a book for the dummies series book, known as Branding Small Business for Dummies. He is the only person in this universe who wrote for both of these inspiring and informative series. He finished the polar race, which is a biennial race from Resolute, Nunavut, in northern Canada to the magnetic North Pole. Its the 650 kilometers footrace pulling food and equipment on sleds. Less than 100 people in the world have successfully completed it. Raymond finished it in APRIL 2007 with a total time of 17 d 4 h 35 min 54 s. REAL WOW! I am the marathon man, who finished not one, but two marathons in one year. I ran my first marathon October 18, 2015 in 6 hrs 22 min 35 sec. I ran my second marathon October 16, 2016 in 6 hrs 3 min. To learn more about my marathons, go to youarethecelebritybook.com. You never know, you might see my book about my marathon experiences. Let me know if you would love to learn more about my marathon runs. Running in a marathon makes me healthy, happy and gives me a chance to inspire you.

Let me bring back you from my marathon to Raymond. I met Raymond more than 10 years ago. One day, I went to one of his motivational seminar. Raymond was one of the speakers. During the presentation, he was looking for a volunteer to read legendary Robert Kiyosaki's book, *Cashflow Quadrant,* because on page 167, Robert mentioned how he benefited through Raymond's services. I associate with the best. You become with whom you associate with. I grabbed the opportunity and read that testimonial for Raymond in front a huge audience. From there onwards, I started to move into the inner circle of Raymond. I started going to most of his seminars in Toronto. I joined his amazing book writing online program, known as the 10-10-10program.com.

I highly encourage you to register ASAP if you are really serious about becoming an author. Raymond has created over a thousand authors all over the world and keeps creating them. It gives me more peace to inspire you to be the author. A book is a legacy. One day I will be gone, but I will be alive through my book to keep inspiring you, 'I CELEBRATE' is my purpose in this universe. The purpose of life is to have a life of purpose. What is your purpose?

Rules:

1. 2 words.
2. First word must be 'I'
3. Second word must be the verb which describes you as a whole.

I MOTIVATE, I HELP, I CREATE, and more.

I thank you for finding your life purpose.

Let me bring you back to Raymond. I have met several motivational speakers through Raymond.

JACK CANFIELD

BOB PROCTOR

DR. JOHN GRAY

DR. IVAN MISNER

MARK McKOY

The list could go on and on. Each of these speakers inspired me to reach for various milestones or to create changes in my life. They can do the same for you, if you are willing to open your mind to the possibilities.

I went to Raymond's yearly retreat in 2016. It was a MSC DIVINA business cruise from Miami, USA, to the BAHAMAS, ST. MARTIN and PUERTO RICO with over 125 of his international clients. I've taken several cruises, even sometimes taking them back to back. That means the day I finished the cruise was the same day I went to on my next cruise. I learned so much during that business cruise. For real life lessons, you should be away from home in the total luxury, and led by a master, through deep life lessons. All four requirements were met during that cruise. While coming back from Miami to Toronto, I was traveling in business class for the second time in my whole life. I was surprised to see Raymond on the same flight. What a coincidence! I was in the third row and he was in the second row. Award winning author Tony Roma, one of my friend Raymond's clients, was in the first row of business class. I was happy to see that the next seat beside him was empty. I requested the seat beside Raymond. He is always generous. He didn't mind. I was on top of the world. His young and beautiful wife Karyn was on the same flight, but she was in the economy class with her parents. I asked Raymond one question. Without sugar-coating it, please tell me how can I reach the same level of success that you have. Raymond pored his heart, his wisdom, and mastermind out from Miami to Toronto flight over thousands of kilometers in the air. I've taken hundreds of flights, but I will cherish this one all my life. Generally, Raymond charges several thousands of dollars for his coaching. He even told the story how he ignored the passenger beside him, but he ended up coaching him for $5000 for less than an hour.

I am really blessed to have the legend Raymond Aaron as my life mentor. May God bless him, his family, his clients and his mission.

Again, I could write several books about Raymond, but I must to stop here about Raymond. I highly encourage you to surround yourself with several spiritual gurus, as well as life mentors. A life without mentors is unfulfilled.

To get your bonuses, please visit:

www.youarethecelebritybook.com or
facebook.com/youarethecelebrity.

Now that you've enjoyed this chapter about my mentors and you've decided to have several mentors in several areas of your life, then let me tell you that you will enjoyy the next chapter for sure. Let's sail together from the sea of sameness to the island of individuality.

I've Murali Murthy as my online business mentor.

www.thecelebrityguru.com password: 1freedom.

Let me know if you are a dreamer and seriously looking to fulfill your dreams by creating your online business. Murali Murthy has written three books.

Mike Shryer is my Facebook guru and the award-winning

author of the book "Facebook Phenomenon", along with several other books.

Phil Richardson, the LinkedIn guru, is my mentor for LinkedIn. Phil is the award-winning author, who delivered a speech at LinkedIn headquarters.

Did you get my point yet? Having several coaches or mentors in your life is the key to success. I went to medical school to study medicine and a homeopathic college to become a homeopathic doctor. I have spiritual mentors to guide me spiritually. I have life mentors for various aspects of my life. I have an online business mentor and one for Facebook. Did you fulfill your dreams yet? Enough is enough. You have one life. That's it. I highly encourage you to have several coaches or mentors in your life to get what you want. I am the celebrity coach. STOP reading right now. Go to youarethecelebritybook. com or facebook.com/youarethecelebrity and message me that you need me as your celebrity coach. You never know, I might actually become your celebrity coach.

CHAPTER 3

BILL CLINTON

B ILL CLINTON IS the celebrity who doesn't need any introduction. When I was in India during the early years of Bill Clinton's presidency in the USA, one of the most powerful countries in the world, I used to read a lot of great articles in the news papers and magazines, as well as listen to the radio about Bill Clinton. I fell in love with his persona, his charisma and more. I mean really fell in love. I desired to meet him. One of my wildest dreams, which was to meet Bill Clinton, had started. Believe in your wildest dreams. Do not let anybody steal your dreams. You are your own worst enemy when it comes to your dreams. You get about 60,000 thoughts a day. How many of them become part of your dreams? Most of those dreams are stolen by you, your family, your relatives, your friends, or even by your enemies. Am I right? Of course, I am right.

On July 23, 1996, destiny brought me to Toronto, Canada, the next-door neighbor to the USA. To go to the USA was my childhood dream. When I saw the wedding invitation for my cousin, I saw Canada instead of the USA. Then I learned that Canada was a separate country. I thought it must be one of the states of USA. I am talking about my knowledge of Canada in 1994. Even though I have lived in Canada for about 20 years, I have been to the USA more than 100 times. The reason I am writing this book is because I want you to believe in your wildest dreams. Dream big dreams. When I got married, I came to the west from the east. I thank VARSHA, the love of my life, for getting married to me. Varsha also gave me the gift of our beautiful son, PREM.

I was going by Greyhound bus from Toronto to Atlantic City, USA, the second biggest gambling city in the world to attend the wedding of my cousin Rekha, who got engaged in India before coming to USA. However, she ended up falling in love with another man of Indian background while working at a casino in Atlantic City. I decided to support her, even though her decision to break off her engagement. All the relatives boycotted the marriage because of orthodox thinking. I believe in LOVE, so I decided to attend to support her LOVE. My bus stopped in New York for several hours. I was able to get off the bus and see a few things in New York. I saw one photo booth. The instructions on the booth said if you want your fake picture with Bill Clinton, Mr. President, then just put in a few dollars and you will get your picture with Bill Clinton instantly. Wow! I was so happy and on top of the world. My wildest dream to meet Bill Clinton was getting closer and closer, becoming more and more clear. I still cherish that picture. I enlarged that picture and laminated it. In fact, as I am writing this, that picture is beside my laptop. Twenty years have passed, but for me, time stops when I see that picture.

Now imagine, what's the probability of me attending a marriage, which was boycotted by family members? What's the probability out of 50 states, that I would end up in New York state, and out of the huge New York State, I would end up downtown New York by the booth, which gave me the opportunity to have a picture with Bill Clinton? By the way, that was the first and last booth I've ever seen, which gave individuals the opportunity to have pic with Bill Clinton. If you love someone so much, the universe creates opportunities for you.

On AUGUST 29, 2009, Bill Clinton came to BMO, CNE ground, Toronto, to deliver a historical speech. I was super excited because finally, after over 15 years, it was time to fulfill my wildest dream to meet my hero Bill Clinton. I bought the CNE ground ticket. I reached to the BMO venue inside CNE to buy the ticket for Bill Clinton's speech, but the event was sold out event. I came to know about this event at the last minute, so I did not have time to buy the ticket in advance. I was looking out from the curtain beside the fence, hoping to see Bill Clinton, but I was not able to see him. I climbed a huge wall and stood on that wall, but I was still not able to see Bill Clinton. I was so eager to see my hero, Bill Clinton. When he was almost done with his speech, I found out how he was going to be leaving. I slept on the road beside the fence. There was the gap between the road and fence. OMG! I saw Bill Clinton, my hero, from that gape. I shouted from top of my lungs, "Mr. Clinton, Canada loves you!" Bill Clinton was about 20 meters away from me, and he was looking for the direction of my voice, and finally, Bill Clinton saw me. Wow! As soon as Bill Clinton saw me, I shouted again from the top of my lungs, "Mr. Clinton, I love you too!" I felt on top of the world. I felt a peace of mind. I cannot adequately describe my feelings through my writings here, but I know you've got a huge, beautiful, awesome heart to understand my feelings. I also saw him while leaving from the gate where I was standing, with his window have down. At the same time, I also met Toronto Mayor David Miller. Dreams do come true, no matter what! As long you are consistent and persistent in following your dreams. Dream big dreams. Believe in your wildest dreams. Do not let anybody steal your dreams.

On November 21, 2011, I found out that Bill Clinton was coming to the Indigo store, in downtown Toronto, to have launch of his book, "Bill Clinton Back to Work". The whole store was closed to the general public, except people who bought his book in advance. When I went at the venue, I saw huge line of people who had already paid for his book. Now they were in line to meet Bill Clinton and get an autographed copy of his book from him. Again, I found out the day that Bill Clinton was arriving in Toronto, so I did not have time to buy his book in advance. I went to the end of the line and stood. Finally, I was able to pay on the spot for a copy of his book, so I did. There was security to make sure no one brought a camera or cell phones inside. I sneaked my camera in and broke the rule, because I was so optimistic that I was going to get a picture with Bill Clinton. I finally took a picture from several meters away with Bill Clinton by making sure that there was not a single security officer or police officer that saw me. That picture is on my Facebook wall. I was getting closer and closer to Bill Clinton, my childhood hero. I cannot express the feeling. You can imagine how I felt. Keep imagining. I touched his feet to pay respect to him for being my hero, for serving the USA for 8 years, and participating in humanitarian work all over the world. Bill Clinton wanted to shake hands with me. I was delighted to shake hands with him. He autographed his book and gave it to me. I cherish his autographed book, as well as those moments.

Wow! I thank you for living that moment with me by reading and imagining it with me. Think about and write down the hero in your life. What are you willing to do to fulfill your wildest dream to meet your hero, especially if it is a hero that you never met? Start your journey to meet your hero and to fulfill your wildest dream.

This is up-branding. You have to understand the concept

of branding first, before you can understand the concept of up-branding. Branding is the promises you keep and the promises you deliver. This is a simple concept, but 97% of people are not branded and that's why they are unsuccessful. There is a bigger celebrity than you. You create the opportunity to take a picture with that celebrity, get the autograph of that celebrity and then market it in such a way that your brand also shines. This is up-branding. When the pope comes to the USA, the President of USA invites the pope to the White House to up-brand himself. Even though the brand of the President of USA is gigantic, all the great companies focus on keeping the brand of their company shining. How about you? I am glad to know that you understood the importance of branding and up-branding.

What I've learned from Bill Clinton is that you can live like a king, no matter your race, religion or position. Do not take your position so seriously. You can put your ego on the side and promote your spouse any position, even as a candidate for President of USA.

I know you would love to hear from me about Bill Clinton's love affair with Monica Lewinsky. What you focus on, it expands. Bill Clinton focused on extra marital affair with Monica Lewinsky, and he got the aftereffect. Let's forgive him, because only the person who has right to judge others has never made a mistake in life themselves. I know you and I have made lots of mistakes in life. Who am I or who are you to judge Bill Clinton's mistakes or someone else's mistakes?

I want you to write down three politicians on your celebrity list. What will you do to fulfill your dream to meet them? What are the qualities that you like about them? I would love to hear about your journey to meet your celebrity. Feel free to go to youarethecelebritybook.com to learn more about me.

Feel free to visit youarethecelebritybook.com, as well as my

Facebook page facebook.com/youarethecelebrity, to get your bonuses.

Now that you've enjoyed my journey to meet my hero Bill Clinton, and how destiny made my wildest dream possible, I am sure that you are eager to read the next very interesting chapter. Am I right? Let's take the ride together.

CHAPTER 4

NARENDRA MODI

NARENDRA MODI IS India's Prime Minister and took office on May 26, 2014. Modi was the winner of the TIME person of the year online poll in 2015, as well as 2016. However, TIME made the "Ebola virus" the person of year on their cover in 2015. How come a virus can become a person? Modi got 18 % of the online vote. Donald Trump got only 9 % of the online vote. How come Donald Trump was the TIME person of the year in 2016?

The story of the rise of India's PM (Prime Minister) is the story of a rising star from a lower middle-class family, whose father used to sell tea at the railway station of Vadnagar, in the Gujarat state of India. Small Narendra use to help his father by selling the tea at the railway station, as well as going to the school. He also joined RSS at a small age. RSS is the Hindu nationalist association formed in 1925 and stands for Rastriya Swayamsevak. He learned lots of life lessons about Hinduism, as well as love for the nation.

You can nickname him the "Crocodile man". Young Modi was an adventurous boy. He used to find crocodile babies while swimming with his friends in the Sharmistha lake in his hometown of Vadnagar. During his preteen years, he once caught a baby crocodile. Modi brought that baby crocodile baby to his home and his mother Hiraben had to emotionally blackmail him to put the baby crocodile back into the lake. She told him just like he would be miserable if he were to be separated from the mother, the same was true of the baby crocodile. Modi agreed to put the baby crocodile back into the lake.

I joined RSS too during my childhood. I enjoyed the outdoor games, as well as learned to respect India during this time.

Modi was engaged at the tender age of 13 and later married to Jashodaben when he was 18. The marriage was never consummated. Modi went to the Himalayas for a couple of years and then became very active in the RSS.

He joined BJP (Bharatiya Janta Party), which was formed in 1980 as the union of Bharatiya Janta Sangh founded by Dr. Shyama Prasad Mukherjee in 1951 and the Janata Party. Narendra Modi was elected as the CM (Chief Minister) of Gujarat, one of the states of India and where Mahatma Gandhi and I were born. He won his forth consecutive term as the CM of Gujarat and eventually served Gujarat for 13 years, becoming the longest serving CM of Gujarat. Modi became the PM (Prime Minister) candidate from the BJP (Bharatiya Janta Party). He revolutionized the Indian election by using social media, motivating the youth of India, as well as delivering several hundred speeches all over India for almost a year. He became the PM of India on May 26, 2014 by getting a majority and by breaking records over 30 years old.

During the first two and half years as India's PM, he has made 56 foreign trips on 6 continents, and visited 45 countries to brand India to the world. He convinced the world to celebrate the 21st of June as the international yoga day. On June 21, 2015, Modi participated in the first international yoga day celebration in Delhi, India. It made the Guinness Book of World Records for the title's largest yoga lesson, as 35,985 people took part.

One day I went to donate blood through religious group called "Swadhyay Parivar" founded by

HH. Pandurang Shastri. I was rejected because 20 years ago I used to live Surat, a malaria endemic area. The first time I heard about Modi was though the swadhyay parivar devotee. I learned that Modi is Gurajrat's very successful Chief Minister (CM). He developed Gujarat very well. I started to learn more about him. Bhavesh, my best friend, is Modi obsessed. My wildest dream to meet Modi was born. U.S. officials denied Modi a visa as he was preparing to travel to New York to address an Indian-American rally scheduled in Madison Square Garden. That decision was based on Modi's failure to stop a series of deadly riots in the Indian state of Gujarat in 2002, but even the Supreme Court of India did not find him guilty. As soon as Modi became the PM of India, the USA spread the red carpet for Modi and he addressed Indian-Americans at the same Madison Square Garden. Dreams do come true. This incidence gave me so much inspiration. I know you will also be inspired by this incident to fulfill your dreams. I was eager to attend that speech, but I was rejected because the amount of people that wanted to meet Modi exceeded the capacity of the venue. My heart was broken, because I wanted to meet my hero. I wanted to fulfill my wildest dream to meet Modi.

The year 2015 came with the great news that my hero Modi was coming to Canada. I was praying to God that he would deliver his speech in Toronto, so I would have a chance to meet my hero Modi and fulfill my wildest dream. God heard my prayer. My union, 42kpsamaj.com, was one of the proud sponsors that brought Modi to Canada. I was a board member of 42kpsamaj.com when it was formed. Finally, April 15, 2015 arrived. Modi was scheduled to address the Indian Canadians at a rally to be held in the Ricoh Coliseum in Toronto. The Ricoh Coliseum also gave me lots of joy during IIFA Rocks 2011. (IIFA is the International Indian Film Academy.) IIFA will be part of chapter 8.

About 2 am, on April 15, 2011, I went with my best friend Bhavesh to the venue where Modi was coming to address more than 10,000 people. I saw people with lots of Indian flags. Some were wearing orange t-shirts with Modi's picture. I went with a huge Canada flag because I knew most would be coming with Indian flags. I lived in Canada almost half of my life. I love India a lot, but I also love Canada too. I started dancing garba (Gujarati folk dancing) with one of the most energetic groups. I didn't learn garba until 2004. I started to do garba after my father Prahladbhai's brother Hargovankaka's daughter Kavita's marriage. I had one older sister Kailash, but I saw her in pictures only, because Kailash died in childhood. Kavita is my cousin, but we were raised as a real brother and sister. I don't what happened but on the wedding day of Kavita, I did garba for several hours. After 2004, I never missed a chance to do garba. I was so shy about doing garba, but my shyness was gone after doing my first garba. It is hard, but not impossible to learn new things. My brother Maheshbhai also joined us to see Modi. Finally, the doors of the venue opened. Wow! I was full of joy to see 10,000 Indo-Canadians, as well as to feel that one of my wildest dreams was about to be fulfilled in couple of hours. My seat was at the last table, so far from the stage. Local dancers started to dance on the stage. Slum Dog Millionaire's Oscar award-winning song "Jai Ho" was sung by singer Sukhwinder Singh, along with several other songs. Finally, the moment had arrived. My wildest dream to see my hero Modi was fulfilled. Modi entered the venue with Namaste pose. Namaste means I honor the place in you in which the entire universe dwells. I honor the place in you which is of love, light, peace and joy.

When you are in that place in you and I am in that place in me, then We Are One.

As soon as Modi entered in the venue, I ran from last seat towards the stage by breaking all the security borders. I found a seat just by the stage in the second row. I felt on top of the world. I know its not right to break the law, but I can't help it. When I see celebrities, I go into a different zone. I am hypnotised by the persona of that celebrity. I went to a different universe. I can not describe that feeling here, but I want you to have that feeling for someone. Write down three celebrities in politics who are alive and that give you the same feeling I just described. Write down what you are willing to do to meet them in person. Write down how you would feel after meeting them. There are more chances to fulfill your dreams if you write them down and visualise that moment several times a day.

Canada's PM Stephen Harper gave a short and sweet speech. I was focused on my hero Modi that I did not know that I was also going to meet Canada's PM Stephen Harper and First Lady Mrs. Laureen Harper.

LET'S GO ON THE SUN.

—DR. PPP, THE CELEBRITY GURU.

Finally, the moment had arrived. Modi was asked to address us. As soon as Modi started to speak, people started to cheer Modi, Modi, Modi, including me. During his speech, there was an arena full of individuals chanting, Modi, Modi, Modi. After the speech, Modi left the stage with PM Harper as well as Mrs. Harper. I wanted to shake hands with Modi. I was a couple feet away from Modi. I was lucky to also shake hands with PM Harper. I still feel the feeling of shaking hands with PM Harper. I was not able to shake hands with Modi. I was a little heart broken, but I was blessed to see him just a couple of feet away. Finally, the wildest dream to meet my hero Modi was fulfilled.

I was interviewed by several TV channels as soon as I came out of the venue. I saw myself in my phone giving an interview while going home the same day. Wow!

I've heard thousands of speakers in my life, but very few know how to communicate. Communication equals intimacy. Modi is definitely one of the best communicators, which is why he is also one of the best speakers. I am an international celebrity speaker. I started delivering speeches when I was less than 10 years old. My father was my first mentor for my speaking career. I also got 3 certificates by attending Raymond Aaron's speakers and communication workshop. Visit youarethecelebrity.com to hire me to speak in your country, as well as if you want to take the celebrity speaker and communication workshop. Communication equals intimacy. Communication equals wealth. Master the art of communication by attending my communication and speakers workshop.

DREAMS DO COME TRUE.

BELIEVE IN YOUR WILDEST DREAMS.

DON'T LET ANYBODY STEAL YOUR DREAMS.

Wow! I am delighted to share my love as well as journey to meet Modi. You enjoyed it a lot. Am I right? I know I am right. You are eager to read the next chapter. Without further delay, let me bring you to the next journey.

CHAPTER 5

DONALD TRUMP

I AM GOING TO share my love for Donald Trump, which started years before anyone knew he would be the 45th president of the USA. You either love him or hate him, but you can not ignore him. That's the proof of the huge TRUMP brand. Branding is everything. One of the reasons Trump won was because of TRUMP brand, which was self made. Trump knows how to market himself. Trump was one of the best connectors. This election was one of the most watched elections in the history of the USA, just because of Trump. One day, I bought Trump's book from Walmart during the election campaign. One of the Walmart employees became so threatened by seeing Trump on the cover of that book. That Walmart employee was so fearful of Trump, even though she was living in Toronto. That was a great example of branding. Branding means promises you keep and promises you deliver. 97 % are unsuccessful because they are not branded. Successful companies are branded. How about you? I want you to be successful. That is why I am sharing the secret of success, the importance of branding. When you are branded, you always shine light on your brand. You shine light on your brand by up-branding. Your association with a higher brand than yours is called up-branding. A U.S. president wants a picture with the Pope. Both have such huge brands, but the U.S. president knows that by having a picture with the Pope, he will be up-branded. The Pope knows by having a picture with the U.S. president, he will keep shining up his brand.

I love big things, such as big celebrities, big cities and more. I was born in JHULASAN, which had a population of about 6,000, but I rarely lived in JHULASAN. I studied about 5 years in Jhulasan, 3 years in SARDHAV, 3 years in PANSAR, 2 years in AHMEDABAD, 9 years in SURAT, and 20 years in TORONTO. All of those places are bigger than JHULASAN.

I have gone to Atlantic City several times, as well as Las Vegas. Again, those two cities are the top two gambling cities in the world. I do not gamble. One of the reasons I have gone, however, is that both cities have huge and colourful buildings (Casinos). Casinos are huge. In both places, I saw a TRUMP casino.

I also have a hobby of collecting books, especially positive mental attitude books, religious books, and autobiographical books. Trump wrote several books. Trump was born into a rich family, but once upon a time, he was in debt and became multibillionaire. I love a warrior who bounces back. I love elegant resorts. Trump built elegant buildings all over the world. There is a Trump Tower in my city of Toronto too.

I found out several months ago that Donald Trump is coming to deliver a speech via satellite through an event held by Learning Annex in Toronto, in March 2008. It was another of my wildest dreams to meet him, so I was super excited to see him via satellite. I was living that moment. I shared this information with my colleagues. Two colleagues asked me to pick them up in my car. A third said he was not sure, but if he was going to come, then he would come by public transportation. Finally, that day arrived. I woke about 4 am. Left home about 4:30 am. I picked up my two colleagues and reached the event at 5:30 am. The venue was just beside CN Tower, Toronto. CN Tower held the record of tallest free-standing structure for over 30 years. Guinness recertified CN Tower as the world's tallest free-standing tower. There was the reason to be there at 5:30 am, even though the event was supposed to start at 8:00 am, because the first 50 attendees were supposed to get $100. I started to count from the first person. I told him did you sleep here or what to be the first? Our numbers were 52, 53 and 54. We were a little disappointed that we didn't make it under 50 to get the $100 each. We were happy, however, because we got to see Trump via satellite. Finally, the doors of the venue opened at 6 am. I upgraded my seat to the VIP, so I had got entry about 7:00 am inside the hall, which has about 100 rows each. The rows were about 40 chairs long, so about 4,000 seats were in that venue. I always love to sit near the stage. I got my seat in the second row in the VIP area. I also saved another 2 seats beside me for my colleagues. About 7:30 am, my two colleagues got entry with the general admission crowd, as the Learning Annex organisers gave us huge balls to play with and to have fun. I started to kick them in the air. I was having so much fun. I went to meet my two colleagues to bring them with me in the second row VIP area, but they didn't want to come because they had general tickets, not the VIP ticket. I finally convinced them to come to the second row by telling them the risk to bring them from the general area to the VIP area is on me. My third colleague called me that came by public transportation. I found him and brought him to the VIP area too, along with another two colleagues. Finally, about 8:00 am, they showed CN Tower and said to auction it. I have so much emotional connection to the CN Tower. I kissed the CN Tower over 100 times. I have seen CN Tower over several thousand times from afar while driving my car. I've been on top of the CN Tower over 10 times. When they told 4000 people to auction it, I knew that they didn't own CN Tower. I actively participated in that auction. I said several million, somebody said several billion then I said 1 trillion. As soon as I said 1 trillion, there was pin drop silence. Nobody dare to go beyond 1 trillion. I got congratulated for winning that auction. One gentleman, who was tall and wearing a professional suit came to me and he congratulated me. He said you won a beautiful property in a gated community in the USA. I told him that I was just having fun. I am not giving you even one penny. He said this is totally free. I make sure with him several times that he understood that I was not going to give them even a penny. He said yes sir. You will get it for free. He said let's go to the back for the paperwork on your property, the one you won. I stood up from my chair in the second row and went all the way behind the last row. I felt top of the world. 4,000 people's 8,000 eyeballs were looking at me. Yes, I won the beautiful land in the resort in Oklahoma, midway between Oklahoma City and Dallas, Texas for FREE. I got approached by several realtors who wanted to buy my property. I told them I just won it, let me enjoy it. One realtor said let me read your papers to make sure. He was impressed to read the papers on my property. I told my brother who did not believe that. He asked how come someone gives away land for free? Varsha, the love of my life, did not even believe this. The next year, Varsha, our son Prem, and I went to our property inside that resort in Oklahoma, USA. The lesson I got is life is full of daring. I dare! Do you dare? Its always best to get out of your comfort zone. People say think outside of the box. Why do you even think that there is the box?

Believe in your wildest dreams. Don't let anybody steal your dreams.

After that auction, the Learning Annex sold several USA

properties, worth more than $30,000, on that day. I came to understand finally that first to get people out of the fear of buying a property in a different country during the huge recession, they did an auction of the first property for free.

During that day, the speaker told all of us to dance and the winner will win an iPod. I did a headstand and crossed my legs at same time on the chair. I was trained to do that by my father Prahladbhai since my childhood, but it was the first time I did it on the chair. I was one of five they chose to dance on the stage in front of about 4,000 people. I did same headstand and cross my legs again. I was the winner out of 4,000 people and I won an iPod. I gifted it to my son Prem.

Finally, the moment had arrived. The moment to see Trump via satellite. I enjoyed that moment with 4,000 people. My goal was to see Donald Trump via satellite, but I end up winning the iPod, as well as FREE land inside a resort in the USA. You never know when God decides to shower his blessings.

To get your bonuses please visit:

youaretheceelbritybook.com and
facebook.com/youarethecelebrity.

You also need celebrity coaching from me to become a celebrity. Let me know if you need The Celebrity Guru as a celebrity speaker in your country.

Visit Youarethecelebritybook.com, as well as facebook.com/youarethecelebrity, for any questions and your bonuses.

You enjoyed learning about my love for Donald Trump. You also enjoyed hearing how I won the property inside the resort in the USA. You are super excited to read the next chapter. The next chapter is one about my childhood hero, whom I respect so much. He is the superstar of the millennium.

On Jan 18, 2017 at about 1 am, I was about to sleep and one

thought came to my mind. What am I doing in Toronto while Mr. Trump's inauguration on Jan 20. This chapter should not end without me attending this inauguration live and seeing it with my own eyes. The next moment, I wrote on all my social media accounts, including Twitter, my personal Facebook page, as well as my three business pages and two my mentors' Facebook groups that The Celebrity Guru, DR. PPP, was going to attend the inauguration. Within about 15 minutes, I got a response from Tanya Ortiz in West Virginia, USA, who is in my mentor Raymond Aaron's Facebook group. Tanya has attended Raymond's event in Baltimore, USA. Tanya said to me, "You are staying to my home. I am about 1 hour from the White House." I had no option but to say yes because of the warmth I felt. Wow! Facebook connects! Facebook rules! Don't take the power of social media granted. I informed my best friend Bhavesh, whom I was supposed to pick up at the Toronto airport next day. I googled MR. TRUMP'S schedule for Jan 19, 20 & 21, 2017. I decided to see Mr. Trump on Jan 19 about 3 pm at Arlington Cemetery in Washington, DC. I packed my bag. I didn't sleep that night because of the excitement. I started driving my car on the same day at about 10 pm and I drove whole night. I reached Tanya's home about 8:30 am. I received a warm welcome by Tanya, as well as Tanya's dog Maxx Ortiz, one of the biggest German Sheppard dogs I've met, as well as 3 beautiful cats. One was totally white, which was the first time I had ever seen that. I heard an interesting story about Tanya's other cat that had passed away. She is one of the best animal lovers I've ever met. After having a lunch of Italian pasta made by Tanya, I started to drive to meet Mr. Trump at Arlington Cemetery. I saw a helicopter that was continuously in the sky for security reasons, making sure everything was safe. I also saw several police cars for security as well. I was so excited to meet Mr. Trump. I saw more than 50 cars arrive at full speed, one after another. In one of the cars, Mr. Trump was sitting with two windows fully open so people got a chance to see him. Wow! I was on top of the world to see Mr. Trump. I decided to attend a 4 pm to 6 pm concert near the White House, but I drove about 2 hours to find the parking. With about 30 kilometers of area being blocked off, I didn't find any parking, so I left for Tanya's home. Tomorrow was the big day, the inauguration day of Mr. Trump. I wanted to attend Mr. Obama's inauguration day, but I missed both times. I was attending an inauguration ceremony for the first time in my life. I went from Canada, but I was so excited because I was ready to share my experience with you. Finally, after 2 sleepless nights, I slept like a baby and left Tanya's home at 5:00 in the morning. I reached the parking at Arlington Cemetery, but today that parking lot was closed. Finally, I ended up at the parking near the Pentagon, which is the headquarters of the United States Department of Defence. The Pentagon is one of the world's largest office buildings with about 6,500,000 sq. ft. and more than 25,000 employees.

On September 11, 2001, exactly 60 years after the building's construction began, American Airlines Flight 77 was hijacked and flown into the western side of the building, killing 189 people. I did a Facebook live from the memorial of those 189 people, which was beside the Pentagon. I decided to park my car in the parking lot of the Pentagon and take the Metro rail to reach the inauguration site. I was going through the tunnel to take the Metro Rail and I saw one police officer checking IDs of the people who were coming towards the Pentagon. I told him that I was from Canada. The police officer told me to move the car to the mall from the Pentagon parking, because only Pentagon employees were supposed to park their car there. I was moving my car out of the parking of the Pentagon and one of the undercover police officers turn on the lights of his car to pull over my car. I stopped my car and got out to go over to his car. He told me to go back to my car. The police officer approached me and told me that I was not supposed to park at the Pentagon. I explained my story. Another officer came. I explained to him too. I was asked for my driver's licence. I gave it to him. I was organising my food and water bottles to carry after parking my car, when the police officer told me not to move in my car. After about 45 minutes, the officer gave my driver licence back and told me that I wasn't going to receive a ticket or a fine. I left the place and parked my car in airport parking and reached to the inauguration place by UBER. UBER is the #1 taxi service and it doesn't own a single taxi. I drove UBER for about a month in Toronto. From driving UBER to being an awarding winning author! Life is full of surprises.

I reached to the inauguration place. I saw lots of people. I bought 2 t-shirts with Mr. Trump's picture and I wore both because I hate to carry extra things. I went through a check point but I felt I was too far from the real inauguration place. I came out from that check point and decided to go to the closest check point. I bought a Donald Trump's red cap, as well as a huge USA flag with Mr. Trump huge picture on it for $20. One New Yorker girl wanted to buy the same cap for $20. I sold it to her and got took for $10. I wore it, as well as the huge flag, like you see Spiderman has behind his back. Imagine! I was wearing Mr. Trump's T shirt, a winter hat and the huge flag. Nobody ignored me. I gave about 20 interviews. I met one retired footballer who used to play for NFL. I also saw people protesting Mr. Trump too. This made me think about real freedom. Can you imagine on the one side Mr. Trump is being inaugurated as the 45th President of the USA and in the same area, thousands of people are protesting? Everybody is expressing their opinions, but I didn't see a single instance of fighting. This is a real democracy. I could not resist doing a Facebook live. I went to the closest check point, but there were lots of people in line. I knew there was no need to stay in line and miss the inauguration. So, I went to the one of the restaurants where I saw the inauguration and I heard it through a huge loudspeaker broadcasting the event live. About 12 pm, I saw the inauguration speech by President Trump. Now Mr. Trump was the official President of the USA. I was on top of the world. I don't have any words to express my feelings. You are very smart, so I leave it up to you to imagine my feelings. I got into the line to see the parade live. I reached it after a check point. As soon as I reached it, I saw lots of cars passing by and in one of the cars was President Trump. One by one different groups of soldiers representing different states of the USA paraded by, taking 3 non-stop hours. I saw groups of soldiers with horses, motor cycles, helicopters, dancing, and marching together in rhythm. Any country, after watching this parade, would never dare to fight the USA. After the parade, I went to the first ballroom, where President Trump was supposed to dance with First Lady Melina Trump. I didn't have a ticket as well as the proper white t-shirt. After trying another ballroom, where I again was denied for not having a ticket or the right attire, I left for Tanya's home. The next day, Tanya booked me for 1 Million March On Washington. I didn't have a chance to see the front of the stage because of there being about 1 million people. I did a Facebook live from there too. I've never witnessed the freedom of expression by 1 million people and everything was running so smoothly. I've seen lots of interesting posters made by people.

I reached Tanya's home after the march. The following day, I had the chance to meet Tanya's parents. Tanya's father represented the USA in tennis internationally. I was ready to play tennis with him, but he was recovering from heart surgery. Tanya's mother showed me the autographs that Martin Luther King had given her personally during her younger days. After meeting them, Tanya and I went to downtown Baltimore. I saw the coliseum of Baltimore, where I went in 2002 to attend a BWW function. In Chapter 10, you will learn more about the BWW. Tanya saw one store that sold hot sauce. We went inside that store. I saw a poster about their hot sauce challenge. I asked more about it and was interested in trying it. I love challenges. Before I started, I had to sign a piece of paper stating I was responsible if anything happened to me. The store person explained about its 3 million hot versus regular sauces. As part of the challenge, I was supposed to put some on a certain part of the tongue. The hot sauce sample was not supposed to touch the tongue. Tanya was doing a Facebook live of my challenge. The store cashier said not to involve her in the picture but as soon as she heard my opening speech for my Facebook live, she was happy to participate in that.

That's how fast a transformation can happen! I was feeling so much burning in my mouth from the hot sauce, but I was on Facebook live, as well as being macho front of Tanya and the store cashier. I didn't shout, but I started sweating profusely because I was not fully expressing my feelings vocally. I was glad to take this challenge on.

The day after the hot sauce challenge, I left Tanya's home at about 9 am to reach Hershey's Chocolate World, which is the headquarters of Hershey Chocolate. I saw the world's biggest chocolate bar. I made my own DR. PPP's chocolate bar and toured Hershey town. About 7 pm that evening, I was driving uphill in the mountains of Pennsylvania on Highway I-81 North and my car lost the control because of freezing rain for about 60 seconds. My car was going from one lane to another without my control. Finally, I was able pull over to the shoulder lane. Next to the shoulder lane, there was a deep valley. I still have no idea how I survived without any accident. I took a rest for about an hour and then started driving again. A short time later, my car got stuck. One driver stopped in the rain and helped me to get my car unstuck. I took an exit to stay overnight in the motel and to bring my car to a repair shop. I saw the motel, but I missed the road, and because of that, I ended up back onto highway I-81 North. I took exit 206 on I-81 in Pennsylvania, USA, and I slept in my car the whole night with the snow, rain, and cold. I would warm up the car for about 15 minutes, then sleep for some time and when I started feeling cold, I would turn the car on and warm it up again. In the morning, I went inside a local convenience store and the owner, who was working that night, was from the same province of India where I was and had the same last name of Patel. You will rarely see any gas station or motel in the USA, which is not owned by a Patel. Once I was once drove my car from Toronto to Florida 26 hours nonstop, except when I stopped to fill the car with gas, and for about an hour at my brother-in-law Mukeshkumar's home to leave my son Prem. At one of those gas stations, I went inside to pay and I met the daughter of my school principal, who was the owner of the gas station. She also said if you stop at the next exit, you will meet my brother too. Lots of my relatives own gas stations. You should be proud of your last name.

I started to drive again in the morning after eating several bananas and about 500 ml of milk. About 11:30 am, my car suddenly broke down, but again I was fortunate enough to pull my car over to the shoulder lane. I called 911 and also called CAA to tow my car to the closest mechanic shop. I also informed my brothers, Prakashbhai and Maheshbhai. I also informed Tanya. Finally, my car was towed to the Ford repair shop. While my car got repaired, I got the chance to visit one of the biggest malls in Scranton, PA. I ate pasta in a restaurant, and I watched a movie. I got my car repaired after paying $1,150 and I reached Canada safely.

I am glad that what I did gave inspiration to this chapter, to have my book inspire you to change your life. This is how success comes. Success is going out of your comfort zone. Success is not the destination. Success is the journey. Make sure you keep humble despite your success. The number of many people who are better off because of your arrival in this universe is the real definition of success, according to me.

This chapter has nothing to do with whether you love Mr. Trump or you hate him. I attended the inauguration day, as well as the protest day. I am definitely sure that you got the point of believing in your wildest dreams. Put more than 100% in to achieve your wildest dreams. God is always there as your savior to help you through by bringing the right people at right time or he just saves you the way I was saved. Keep counting your blessings.

Please visit www.youarethecelebritybook.com, as well as my Facebook page facebook.com/youarethecelebrity, to get your bonuses and to connect with me if you are looking to have me as your celebrity coach or to have me as a celebrity speaker in your country.

I am sure that you are eager to read the next chapter about my #1 Bollywood celebrity.

CHAPTER 6

AMITABH BACHCHAN

AMITABH BACHCHAN IS the superstar of the millennium. He is also known as the Shahenshah of Bollywood. I never met any Indian who did not watch his movies. Amitabh is my favorite movie hero. I started to dream through him. I watched his hundreds of movies multiple times. I mimicked him a lot. Who's your favourite movie hero? He is not only famous in India, but also internationally. He has also done a Hollywood movie too. His statue is in several Madame Tussauds museums all over the world.

Amitabh Bachchan won more than 200 awards. In October 2003, TIME magazine dubbed Amitabh Bachchan "The Undisputed Godfather of Bollywood". He has been honoured with an Honorary Doctorate by almost 10 universities around the world.

His father, Harivansh Rai Srivastava, was a celebrity poet. After getting his PhD at Cambridge University, he used Bachchan as his last name instead of Srivastava. Harivansh Rai Bachchan has great relationship with Mr. Nehru, India's first PM and Mahatma Gandhi, who gave the world the gift of truth, nonviolence and freedom. Amitabh decided to become a politician to support his friend Rajiv Gandhi, who was the son of Indira Gandhi, India's PM when Mr. Nehru's daughter Indira Gandhi, died. After a number of years, he left politics when he realized that it was not for him.

He sent his picture into one of the competitions in Mumbai, but he was rejected. He went to Mumbai to act in the movies. His first movie came in 1969 and still he is going strong with his movies. He has acted in more than 150 movies. He was known as an angry young man, because he was representing the common man of India. He also got a great combination of directors, producers, writers, and singers, as well as co-stars. In the beginning, several of his movies did not do well. He was at the railway station of Mumbai and ready to quit Bollywood, when director Prakash Mehra cast him in the movie Zanjeer, which made him star. After Zanjeer, he never ever thought to leave Bollywood.

My two younger brothers Prakashbhai & Brijeshbhai memorized Amitabh's movie Sholey, so that even if you turned off the volume, they could still say every line of dialogue in that movie. I did mimicry of Amitabh on the stage several times.

When I heard that Amitabh was coming to do a show in Toronto, I was thrilled. I went to the venue several hours early. I found out the way Amitabh was supposed to come. I waited for several hours. Finally, he arrived in one of the best cars. He got out of the car and waved his hand towards me. I was on top of the world. I enjoyed his show.

I found out that Amitabh was again coming to do an "Unforgettable Tour" on July 18, 2008 at the Rogers Center, Toronto, near the CN Tower. I was supposed to go to the USA, but I made my plans in such a way that I watched his show and then the next day, I went to the USA. He came with his son Abhishek Bachchan, who is also a Bollywood star. Aishwarya

Rai Bachchan is also a Bollywood star as well as Miss World 1994. Amitabh Bachchan's son Abhishek, as well as Aishrwarya, were on the famous The Oprah Winfrey Show too, along with Bollywood stars Akshay Kumar, Ritesh Deshmukh, music director Vishal and Shekhar.

Shekhar was performed during the "Unforgettable Tour". I still remember the dialogues Amitabh performed during that tour.

Amitabh Bachchan is also very active on social media. Over the last 3200 days, he wrote a blog. On my birthday, I wrote a comment on Amitabh's blog, asking him to wish me a Happy Birthday. He gets thousands of comments daily, but he read mine. Amitabh Bachchan wished me Happy Birthday, even though there was flood in Mumbai, which involved his bungalow. I was surprised to be wished a happy birth day by my hero Amitabh Bachchan. I have celebrated a lot of birthdays and will celebrate many more, but Amitabh Bachchan's birthday wish is something I will always remember. He has lots of great qualities, but his humbleness and the way he connects with you is very impressive. It is not about how much you know, it is about how much you care.

In his movie "PAA", he played a 13 years old boy suffering from progeria. At that time, Amitabh's real age was 67. Amitabh Bachchan became the son of his real son Abhishek Bachchan. I never ever seen a movie except "PAA" in which there was a role reversal of a real-life father and son.

One day I was sending my pictures to my brother Brijeshbhai in India of me with Bollywood actress Esha Deol as well as Bollywood actor Zayed Khan. My uncle asked me through my brother Brijeshbhai to show him my picture with Amitabh Bachchan. I took that challenge and decided I was going to have my picture taken with Amitabh Bachchan. I love challenges. I thank my uncle for giving me this challenge. Are you going to wish me luck in order to fulfill this huge challenge? I know your answer is yes.

One day, a journalist asked Amitabh Bachchan why he hadn't written his autobiography. Amitabh answered gently that he would have to mention himself frequently, which is something that he didn't like to do. The person himself is an institution, but he is not egocentric.

He opened ABCL, Amitabh Bachchan Corporation Ltd. ABCL didn't do well. He went into debt. He started to act for the first time in a TV program called "Kaun Banega Crorepati", the Indian version of "Who wants to be a millionaire?" He brought a revolution in TV. Lots of Bollywood stars started to have their TV shows. He went to director Yash Chopra to ask for a role in a movie. He got the role in Yash Chopra's movie Mohabbatein and the rest is the history. Yet, Amitabh never has an ego.

Amitabh Bachchan has never ever has an affair in the almost half of century of his movie career, except with his movie star wife Rekha. Bollywood is full of glamour and he has been ruling Bollywood for almost 50 years and living the life of lotus is itself a miracle.

On July 26, 1982, Amitabh Bachchan sustained a severe injury while he was shooting a fight sequence with Puneet Issar for Manmohan Desai's movie "Coolie" at Bangalore, India. He was supposed to fall on the table but he miss-timed the jump and hit his abdomen on the edge of the table, which caused internal bleeding. He was flown to Mumbai to be treated at Breach Candy Hospital. The nation mourned and fans prayed for him. That accident left him clinically dead for a few minutes. From that day onwards, he always comes out of his Mumba home every Sunday to meet his thousands of fans to show gratitude to his fans for praying for him when he was on his death bed in the hospital. It is one of my wildest dreams to see Amitabh

Bachchan on a Sunday at his home in front of his thousands of fans.

You can learn several life lessons from Amitabh Bachchan, including persistence, dedication, kindness, hope, golden heart, improvisation, the show must go on and so much more.

I up-branded myself by seeing Amitabh Bachchan, as well as other great celebrities live. I also up-branded myself by copying Amitabh's deep voice. I highly encourage to brand yourself. 97 % people are not branded, so they are unsuccessful. After branding yourself, keep polishing your brand. I also highly encouraging to up-brand yourself by meeting the celebrities.

Learn the techniques of branding and up-branding by visiting youarethecelebritybook.com, as well as joining my Facebook page, facebook.com/youarethecelebrity.

You've enjoyed learning about my love for my hero Amitabh Bachchan. Write down three movie celebrities you would love to meet. What are you willing to do to meet them? How would you feel if you met them? I wish you all the best for your journey to up-brand yourself by meeting your favourite movie star, getting autographs, photographs and interviews with them. As you know, I am The Celebrity Guru. I met over a thousand celebrities in different fields all over the world. If I can do it, you can do it too. Just do it now. Believe in your wildest dreams. Don't let anybody steal your dreams.

You've enjoyed this chapter. Now you are eager to read the next chapter, so without further delay, let me present the next chapter to you.

CHAPTER 7

SHAH RUKH KHAN

SHAHRUKH KHAN IS known as the Badshah of Bollywood. He has appeared in almost 100 movies. He won over 250 awards. A life-size wax statue of Shah Rukh Khan was installed at Madame Tussauds wax museums in London, Hong Kong and New York. Newsweek named him one of the 50 most powerful people in the world. He is not only one of the best Bollywood actors, but also a movie producer, and occasionally, he sings in Bollywood movies too. There are three main khans in Bollywood, Shah Rukh Khan, Salman Khan and Aamir Khan. I'm honoured and humbled to meet all of them who worked over 75 years combined over in Bollywood. In the previous chapter, I introduced Amitabh Bachchan who worked almost 50 years out of 100 years of Bollywood history. Bollywood, Cricket, Spirituality, History and Politics are the main pillars of India.

Shah Rukh Khan's mother used to tell him that you look like the Tragedy King of Bollywood Dilip Kumar, who lost his parents during his teens. Shah Rukh Khan decided to be huge on the earth, so his parents see him from heaven. This is one of his secrets and why he is such a workaholic. Work is worship for him. He knows how to brand himself. How to brand his product, which is his movies. I learned a lot about branding from him. When his latest movie is about to be released, he works day and night to promote his movie. He is also innovative in his ideas.

One day I was working in downtown Toronto and my brother Maheshbhai called to let me know that Shah Rukh Khan was in Toronto. I googled to find out the location and then I found out that he is in Toronto to premiere his move "Ra. One". First, I took a break from my work and went to the premiere. The movie was playing in the dark, so I did not have chance to meet Shah Rukh Khan. I went to his hotel and I saw him going from the hotel to sitting in the car with "Ra. One" movie director Anurag Kashyap. I was about 1 foot away from him. I was mesmerized by him. I waved to Shah Rukh Khan. He waved back to me. I felt great. He went to the club to promote his movie. I went to the club to see him again. I felt on top of the world.

Shah Rukh Khan born in Delhi, India's capital. He lost his parents during his teen years. His acting coach Barry John trained him at the acting school in Delhi. The right coach makes you successful.

If you are the serious about having a coach, I am the celebrity coach. Visit www.youarethecelebritybook.com, as well as my Facebook page facebook.com/youarethecelebrity, to get my coaching services.

Khan falls in love with a Hindu family girl named Gauri. He finally won the hearts of Gauri's family and got married to Gauri. He was a TV star in the beginning. Then he moved to Mumbai. His first movie "Deewana" in 1992 was a huge success. He is a risk taker. He played negative roles in several movies at the beginning of his career. He is innovative. He dares! Whatever he does, he puts his soul, body and mind into it.

Shah Rukh Khan's father was a highly-educated man but poor. Because his father didn't have any money on Shah Rukh Khan's birthday, his father used to give him old things and through those he learned many important lessons. The first old thing his father gifted him with was a chess set. First and foremost, chess taught him cooperation and teamwork. Second, in life, when you have to go forward, there are also times when you do have to take a step backwards too. Third, that even small people, so called pawns, should be respected. No one is small. Everyone is useful. The last thing was that sometimes the things that we love the most, like the queen in chess, may have to be sacrificed.

The second thing that his father gifted him with was the typewriter. When you type something wrong, it becomes very difficult to remove it. So, you should be very diligent and very careful. Whatever you do in life, do it diligently. Do it in a way so that there are no mistakes. Do it with the mindset that this is your first and last chance to do it and you will never get a chance to do it again.

The third life lesson was taught to him by his father's old camera. It never functioned. He could see from the viewfinder but couldn't click to take a picture. Our creativity or hobby can't always become our work. Very few people are fortunate enough to make it. But whatever our creativity is, be it poetry, painting, singing, or dancing, it is not necessary that the world should accept it. Like the camera he had, it couldn't click but whatever one saw through it was beautiful. Similarly, you should hone your creativity for yourself and it doesn't matter whether the world accepts it or not. Because in life when you are alone or depressed, it is your creativity that becomes your best friend whether the world likes it or not.

The forth and final lesson given by his father was the need to have a sense of humour. Always have a child-like innocence.

SHAH RUKH KHAN'S FACEBOOK STYLE 15 LIFE
LESSONS FOR YOU.

1. Do what you like and like what you do. Success will follow.

2. Be the person everybody wants to be friend with or be prepared to be unfriended.

3. Stick to Timelines.

4. Give, give until it hurts.

5. Be Good and Gracious.

6. Keep Silent, and be thought of as a fool, then to open your mouth and remove all doubts.

7. Comment only when need be, when you know enough.

8. Do the right things always and you'll earn the right tag!

9. Do not judge people by their group.

10. n application of mind, body and soul is a must.

11. Build a wall around you to block negativity.

12. Guys, don't stalk girls whom you want to like you back.

13. Girls, just don't report boys if they don't meet your high standards of love that the King Khan has set.

14. Let your interest instill creativity.

15. Never, never, never lose your cool.

10 LIFE LESSONS SHAH RUKH KHAN TAUGHT US IN HIS HONORARY DOCTORATE SPEECH ON THE 15th of OCTOBER 2015 FROM UNIVERSITY OF EDINBURG.

1. Don't become a philosopher before you become rich.

2. Study hard. Work hard. Play harder. Don't be bound by rules. Don't hurt anybody, and never ever live somebody else's dream.

3. It's ok to be confused. Confusion is the route to all the clarity in the world.

4. If you aren't charged up about doing something, if you don't have what in Hindi we call the "Josh" the fire in your belly for it, then don't do it.

5. There's no such thing as 'normal'. That's just another word for lifeless. Madness (of the particular nice/ romantic kind) is an absolute prerequisite to a happy and successful life. Don't ever treat your little insanities as if they are aberrations that ought to be hidden from the rest of the world. All the most beautiful people in the world, the most creative, the ones who led revolutions, who discovered and invented things, did so because they embraced their own idiosyncrasies.

6. Art is more important than the artist-have no attachment to your own art. It's regressive, move on.

7. Whatever it is that is pulling you back, it is not going away unless you stand up and start forging your own path with all your might in the opposite direction. Stop whining and start moving.

8. Live now, Live today. Don't be bound by rules, live your own dream.

9. Being brave means being shit-scared all the way to the party but getting there and doing the 'Funky Chicken' in front of all your teenage kid's friends anyway. Don't let fears becomes boxes that enclose you. Open them up, feel them and turn them into the greatest courage you are capable of. I promise you, nothing will be wrong. But if you live by fears, everything that can possibly go wrong will go wrong and you won't even have done the 'Funky Chicken'.

10. Life is like the Bollywood movie. Everything will be fine in the end. If it's not fine, then it is not the end yet. The movie didn't finish yet.

To get your bonuses go to youarethecelebritybook. com, as well as joining my Facebook page facebook.com/ youarethecelebrity.

Write down your three favourite movie stars. What will you do to fulfill your wildest dreams to meet them. How would you feel? Believe in your wildest dreams. Don't let anybody steal dreams. If Trump can win, so can you. Let me bring you to the next very exciting chapter of my book.

CHAPTER 8

IIFA 2011 & IIFA 2014
INTERNATINAL INDIAN FILM
ACADAMY

IIFA 2011

IIFA IS STANDS for the INTERNATIONAL INDIAN FILM ACADAMY. The IIFA is a unique Bollywood awards ceremony, because the venue must be anywhere in the world except India. I never ever heard another award ceremony in any other country that are held in different countries of the world. The first IIFA was held at the Millennium Dome, London. IIFA is basically about a week of Bollywood celebration every June anywhere in the world except India. Hundreds of all the Bollywood celebrities go to that country and colour it with Bollywood style. It brings two countries together. Brings love, peace, harmony, and creativity together. One of the best excuses to meet an NRI (Non-Resident Indian). You can bring NRI out of India, but you can never bring INDIA out of the NRI. You should love your motherland. You should be always grateful to your motherland. ATTITUDE OF GRATITUDE.

Bollywood is in my body, mind and soul. Bollywood made me dream big. My uncle Mohankaka owned the 'Chirag' movie theater about 10 kilometers from my birthplace Jhulasan. I watched thousands of movies for free at different places in the 'Chirag' movie theater, including the projector room. I also saw my uncle Hargovankaka multiple times in the movie "PUTRAVADHU". My dreams became so huge after that. If my uncle could get into a movie and become huge, so could I.

In January 2011, I knew that the IIFA was coming to North America. With it's three countries, Canada, the USA and Mexico, I was praying that God would bring the IIFA to Canada, instead of one of the other countries. I was also praying the IIFA to come to Toronto where I had now lived for over half my life. The power of prayer is immense, because my prayers were answered. The first time the IIFA came to North America and the venue was Rogers Center, near the CN Tower, Toronto. I was on top of the world. When I learned that the IIFA was coming to Toronto, I also found out that the tickets for the IIFA 2011 were sold out in about 10 minutes. I was heartbroken. God, how could you do that to me, the Bollywood lover boy, The Celebrity Guru, DR. PPP. I didn't lose hope. I finally found two tickets, one for me and one for my relative as well as friend Ronak, through ebay.ca online. The date was June 15, 2011. About one week before that, I went to the Toronto Airport with Ronak to pick up Ronak's uncle, who was coming from India. During our wait for his flight, Ronak told me that they were blocking a certain part of the airport off and there were huge IIFA posters. As soon as I heard that from him, I knew that Bollywood celebrities has started to arrive for IIFA 2011. I told Ronak that I would be staying at the Toronto Airport to meet the Bollywood celebrities. I saw Bollywood celebrities that day as well as the next several days that I was at the airport. I was also at their hotel Fairmount Royal York Hotel. Night time was when I would go to my work. From work, I would go directly to the airport or the Fairmount Royal York Hotel during the IIFA 2011 event. Ronak ended up not being able to attend with me, but Bhavesh, my best friend, decided to join me. He also started to come with me to the Fairmount Royal York Hotel to meet the Bollywood celebrities. I was walking on a cloud. I was on top of the world. I had seen almost 50 Bollywood celebrities at the airport and at the Fairmount Royal York Hotel. One day, I went inside a room full of journalists from around the world and then went to the second row. The first row was full of celebrities, such as Jermaine Jackson (Michael Jackson's brother), Slum Dog fame MR INDIA Anil Kapoor, Bipasha Basu, Boman Irani, Ritesh Deshmukh, Diya Mirza, Mallika Sherawat, and the Consulate General of India, as well as Ontario's premier Dalton Mcguinty. I was on top of the world. This event was not for the general public, like me, but I couldn't resist the temptation to meet those Bollywood celebrities. Now on the stage, Mr. Premier, Anil Kapoor, Bipasha Basu, and the Consulate General of India Toronto presented a cheque by CIBC bank to IIFA. I rushed beside the stage and I took my picture with all those celebrities on the stage as the background of my picture. When all the journalists of the world were taking pictures of the celebrities on the stage, I was taking my picture with all those celebrities in the background. The huge body builder security officer approached to me and asked for my journalist ID. I am not the journalist, so he gently said to leave the room. I didn't mind leaving the room, because I had lived the moment of a life time. No one can take those moments from me, except God. My question to you is have you truly lived all the moments of your life time? After several years, I met the same security officer who told me to leave the room. I reminded him about that same incident. He requested that I tell his boss about the incident and so I did.

One day, there was the session about the movie "Tell Me O kkhuda" in a small room. I went to that room. I saw Bollywood celebrities Dharmendra, Hema Malini, Esha Deol, and Rishi Kapoor. I was on top of the world. When that session finished, I went in the small room where Dharmendra, Hema Malini and Esha Deol went with some cameramen. WOW! I was confused about whom to see first because all of them were being interviewed by three different interviewers. I finally focused on Dharmendra. I still couldn't believe that I was in this small room, just a couple of feet away from the HE-MAN OF Bollywood Dharmendra. His wife was dream girl actress Hema Malini and their daughter was actress Esha Deol. The interviewer was a young gentleman who had just started his interview. Dharmendra didn't satisfy the requirements of the interviewer for the introduction, so he had him do it again. Occasionally, I looked over at Hema Malini, as well as Esha Deol too. I was on a cloud. I was on top of the world.

I've also attended one session with the music director Shankar, Ehsaan, and Loy. Shankar is Hindu. Ehsaan is Muslim. Loy is Christian. Wow! What a great example of world peace! There was also a Bollywood lyricist, writer Javed Akhtar, as well as his wife actress Shabana Azmi. I learned a lot during that session about how divinely the Bollywood songs are created.

Finally, June 14, 2011 had arrived. That was the evening of IIFA ROCKS 2011 at Ricoh Coliseum, Toronto, the same venue where I saw Modi, India's PM, as well as Canada's PM Stephen Harper. I bought tickets for me as well as my other three friends, including Bhavesh. Green Carpet was there. The Bollywood celebrities had started to arrive in awesome cars. I loved the energy of the thousands of fans as soon as they saw the Bollywood celebrity. I was just beside the huge board where the Bollywood celebrities were giving autographs as well as being interviewed, one of the best positions. As soon as

Shahrukh Khan has arrived, the maximum amount of shouting and cheering occurred and it was full of energy. I was fortunate enough to shake hands with Shah Rukh Khan for the first time of my life and I was on cloud nine. I was on top of the world.

I enjoyed IIFA Rocks 2011. Lots of Bollywood performances by Bollywood celebrities, fashion shows by Bollywood celebrities, and a tribute to King of Pop Michael Jackson by his brother Jermaine Jackson and Bollywood singer Sonu Nigam was amazing too. As soon as the show finished, I rushed to the main stage and the chair with Shah Rukh Khan written on it. I took out that paper with his name written on it, then sat on that chair like I was the king. I felt like I was walking on a cloud. I felt on top of the world. Can you imagine? I sat in the same chair where King Khan Shah Rukh Khan had sat!

Finally, the real day June 15, 2011 has arrived. The moment I've been waiting almost half a year for had arrived. I went to Fairmount Royal York Hotel. I met several celebrities, including Bret Lee, the Australian cricketer. My best friend Bhavesh was with me at that time. Bhavesh told Bratll "Say Hi to Schain" (Schain Tendulkar is known as God of cricket, one of the best cricketers the world has ever seen, who has broken hundreds of records, including 100 centuries). I was privileged to meet Schain Tendulkar too. You will have to wait for the next book for that story of my life.

Now finally the time had come for the Bollywood celebrities to go to the Rogers Center for IIFA 2011. I stood at the corner by the Fairmount Royal York Hotel, where all the cars of the Bollywood celebrities have to pass with a low speed. I've seen several celebrities from only a few feet away from me. Finally, I saw Bollywood actress Diya Mirza. Diya rolled the window down and Diya said to me out of hundreds cheering, "I KNOW YOU!". WOW! Bollywood actress Diya Mirza said to me, "I KNOW YOU!" I was on cloud nine. I was on top of the world.

After that, I was super excited. The rush came back. The police officer could not handle my excitement, and told me to leave the place. Anyway, I had the best moments of my life. I went towards the venue of IIFA 2011 Rogers Center, Toronto. About 9 pm, the show started. I was amazed to see hundreds of celebrities, as well as Hollywood celebrities, such as Hillary Swank. When Anil Kapoor came on the stage, I shouted so loudly his favourite word "JHAKAAS" out of 20,000 people that Anil Kapoor replied by saying "JHAKAAS". I was walking on a cloud. I felt on top of the world. The show finished about 2 am. I went to the Fairmount Royal York Hotel after the show. I saw all the Bollywood celebrities coming back to the hotel. I also saw Shah Rukh Khan with one hand shaking hands with audience members and holding a cigarette with the other. What the lovely attitude of gratitude! Did you enjoy my life journey during IIFA 2011? I know you enjoyed my journey a lot. Are you ready to experience real life IIFA?

IIFA 2014

I found out that IIFA 2014 was once again coming to North America. This time IIFA 2014 had decided to come to the USA, in Tampa, Florida. How could I miss IIFA 2014? My brother Prakashbhai decided to come from South Carolina. I decided to go from Toronto by plane. I was super excited, so I bought a business class air ticket for the first time in my whole life. I went to the airport early, so I got to enjoy the lounge. I enjoyed the food, as well as special seating at the lounge area. I also enjoyed an early check in for business class. I was in the first seat of first row. WOW! I took several selfies. I loved the feeling of me sitting on the first seat of the plane and everybody was going behind me. I enjoyed the huge space in business class. It was the first time I was given an iPad to use by a flight attendant.

Special snacks were provided, as well as special food. I enjoyed every moment. I felt Tampa, USA, arrived so fast. I hired a car and went to my hotel by the sea. I went several days early. I went to the hotel of Bollywood celebrities, as well as the venue of the IIFA 2014. Bollywood celebrity Ranveer Singh took my phone from me and he took my picture with him, then gave my phone back to me. WOW! I've met over thousand celebrities in several fields in several countries, but I had never seen this kind of friendly gesture in my whole life. I also attend the question and answer session in a small room with Slum Dog Millionaire fame Bollywood actor Anil Kapoor, and Sholey movie director Ramesh Sippy, as well as actress Alia Bhatt's uncle director Mukesh Bhatt, and IIFA producer Joseph Sabbah.

On April 22, 2014, IIFA ROCKS 2014 had arrived. I reached the venue. I met my brother Prakashbhai, as well as other relatives. Prakashbhai and I ate pizza in the field sitting by a tree, the way we used to eat at our farm in India. Childhood memories came alive. The Bollywood stars started to walk on the red carpet. I was enjoying it, but it didn't satisfy me to see the Bollywood celebrities from afar. I jumped the fence and went closer to the celebrities. I shook hands with several Bollywood celebrities, and I got lots of autographs. I've also met Milkha Singh, also known as The Flying Sikh, who is a former Indian track and field sprinter. In 1958, Milkha Singh set records for the 200m and 400m in the national game in India, held at Cuttack, and also won gold medals in the same event at the Asian Games. He then won a gold medal in the 400m competition at the 1958 British Empire and Commonwealth Games with a time of 46.6 seconds. Bhaag Milkha Bhaag is a movie based on Milkha Singh won several awards in IIFA 2014.

I was interviewed by several channels about India's upcoming election. I promoted Narendra Modi during those interviews during IIFA red carpet. Narendra Modi won the 2014 election and became the PM of India. You read about PM Modi in Chapter 3.

Finally, April 23, 2014 the IIFA day had arrived. My brother Prakashbhai and I got our seats. I wasn't satisfied with the seats we had gotten. I found a closer seat. My brother Prakashbhai and I enjoyed the better view. Finally, the show started with the great entry of the hosts, Bollywood actor Shahid Kapoor and multitalented Farhan Akhtar, who is the Bollywood actor, director, producer, singer, lyricist and host. Now it was time for the entry of Ranveer Singh, which was only a few feet away from my seat on the bike. I loved it. I was on cloud nine. I was on top of the world. I was so happy because for the first time my brother Prakashbhai was with me.

Finally, my wildest dream to see IIFA 2014 ended. The golden moments of IIFA 2014, I will cherish all of my life. It was my pleasure to share it with you. Believe in your wildest dreams. Don't let anybody steal your dreams. Just do it now. If Trump can win, so can you.

Visit youarethecelebritybook.com to get your bonuses, as well as my Facebook page facebook.com/youarethecelebrity. Let me take you away from Bollywood in the next chapter, where I talk about my experiences with sports celebrities.

CHAPTER 9

CRICKET & TENNIS CELEBRITIES

CRICKET CELEBRITIES

C RICKET IS A religion in India. Bollywood and cricket are the two main sources of entertainment in India. You've enjoyed the last three chapters about Bollywood. Are you ready to know more about my life related to cricket? I know you are ready. I am ready too.

When I was in my early teens, my friend Vishnu from Jhulasan, my hometown, told me about the cricket commentator Sushil Doshi's welcome speech for the radio cricket commentary listeners. I started to listen it and I loved it. While listening the crick commentary, I became a master in scoring. During big tournaments, I used to be the scorer who had to write balls to balls. I loved to say the score when someone ask about it. I also hid my fear of facing a real cricket ball, which is hard and consists of a cork center covered by leather. I loved to play cricket with tennis balls only. I loved to bat. I don't love to bowl.

During my medical college time in Surat, India, I found out that Indian cricketers were coming to the Lalbhai Contractor

Stadium to play cricket. I was so excited. I was walking on a cloud. I was on top of the world. One of my friends brought a camera from his relatives for this event. It was the first time that I operated a camera in my life, because generally the camera was handled by my brother Maheshbhai.

I went to the venue. I had never seen so many cricketers in person whom I used to see on the TV as well as hearing them on the radio. I saw Praveen Amre and Sanjay Manjrekar, as well as the God of cricket, Schain Tendulkar. I also saw their coach Ramakant Acharekar. I was walking on a cloud. I was on top of the world. I enjoyed live cricket. After the game finished, one stranger offered to let me meet with Kiran More. I was so excited. He also wanted me to drive his Suzuki or Honda bike, although I don't remember the specific brand. I told him I know how to drive a scooter, because my father had a scooter, but I didn't know how to drive a Suzuki or Honda bike. He explained everything to me in about 5 minutes and he gave me the key to ride it and told me to follow his bike. My excitement to meet Kiran More was so intense that the fear of driving a Suzuki or Honda bike never came into my mind. I enjoyed riding that bike. I finally reached the inside of Kiran More's room. I couldn't imagine that the cricketer I saw from so far playing cricket on the ground was now just a few feet away from me and I was in his hotel room. I felt so shy that not a single word came out of my mouth. I felt like I was in a deep sleep and watching a beautiful dream. WOW!

I shared this experience with my medical student friends and they loved it. The next day, I went to the grounds where those cricketers went for cricket practice. I went inside the grounds and took lots of pictures with all those Indian famous cricketers. I was so happy to shake hands with them and take so many pictures with them. I was walking on a cloud. I felt on top of the world. I went to the picture development store. I gave that camera to the lady to remove the roll and develop it. The lady opened the camera, but omg the camera was empty. There was no roll in the camera. I was operating camera for first time in my life, because I didn't have opportunity to handle the camera. My brother Maheshbhai was the master at operating the camera. I was heartbroken, because for the first time in my life, I had captured magical moments with cricket celebrities and because of a small technical mistake the proof of those magical moments disappeared. When I was clicking the camera, I saw the number was increasing. I shared that incident with my medical student friends too. They still remember this incident.

I went to watch The Sahara Cup played in Canada between India and Pakistan during 1996, 1997 and 1998. I enjoyed those days, feeling on top of the world and as if I was walking in the clouds.

I also went to watch Asian 11 versus Rest of the World cricket match at Rogers Center near CN Tower, Toronto. I went with a huge Indian flag with Indian leather hat. I saw several international crackers, e.g. Maninder Singh, Duleep Mandis, Arjuna Ranatunga, Rohan Sunil Gawaskar, Simmons, Madan lal. Ashok Malhotra, Wasim Akram, Narendra Hirwani, Venkatesh Prasad and more.

I also went at the same venue to watch cricket with international cricketers. I also went to their hotel and personally met Senath Jayasuriya, Brendon McCullum, Tim Southee and many more.

I also went to King City near Toronto to watch T20 cricket between Pakistan, Sri Lanka, Canada, and Zimbabwe. I witnessed Mahela Jayewardene, who was the captain of Sri Lanka team, bringing water for one of his cricketers who was thirsty. This surprised me, but taught me the lesson that you become the leader by serving the team and at the same time, putting ego on the side. After the event, I went to the hotel where those cricketers stayed. I saw Shoaib Malik, the Pakistan team captain at that time, who was married to famous Indian tennis player Sania Mirza. Shoaib Malik was taking the elevator with his other Pakistani cricketers, when I approached to get his autograph. He let the elevator go with his Pakistani cricketers because he was busy giving an autograph to me. This incidence taught me the lesson of being humble by connecting with a fan. I decided that I would stay to give autographs or take pictures with my fans patiently.

I was fortunate enough to stay for one week near Bradman Museum, the international cricket hall of fame in Boral, South of Sydney, Australia. Sir Donald Bradman, whose test batting average of 99.94, is often cited as having the greatest achievement by any sportsman in any sport, according to Wikipedia. "SIR" is the title given by the English royal family, to those who are part of the knighthood. There have been only 20 cricketers in that group, while 8 others got it for service to a different field.

One of my wildest dreams was to meet legendary cricketers Kapil Dev and Sunil Gawaskar. Who is your favourite cricketer? Sachin Tendulkar, The God of Cricket, is my favourite cricketer.

I can promise you that I can keep sharing my experiences about cricket, because cricket is my favourite game. I am now going to share my experiences about my second favourite game, tennis. I know are you ready to start the journey of my love for tennis.

Tennis Celebrities

I am ready to bring you to my journey with tennis. You are ready too. Let's start our journey. I fell in love with watching Tennis just because every year in August there is Rogers Cup for Tennis in Toronto, like the US Open and Australian Open.

You know that I am the celebrity guru who met over thousand celebrities in different fields from several countries. Every year for more than 15 years, I go to watch the Rogers Cup in Toronto, my hometown since 1996. I would love to meet you when you are in Toronto, Canada. You can meet me through youaretheceelbritybook.com too. Imagine now that you are reading my book from somewhere in the world. Just Postulate to meet me, The Celebrity Guru, and the universe make this happen. Postulate is getting the results in physical world by, saying, writing or thinking about what you need. Postulate is more than a thousand times stronger than manifest.

The Rogers Cup is a 10-day event in Toronto, as well as in Montreal, Canada. During Rogers Cup International, tennis celebrities come from all over the world. I was fortunate enough to meet lots of tennis celebrities. The following are a few out of hundreds of tennis celebrities I have met over the last 15 years. I am mentioning them to let you know that if I can do it, you can do it too.

Pete Sampras
Andre Agassi
Jim Courier
Roger Federer
Andy Roddick
Sarina Williams
Martina Hingis
Monica Seles
Mary Pierce
Milos Raonic
Sania Mirza
Mary Pearce
Caroline Wozniacki
& more

One day I was watching Rogers Cup about 15 years ago and I saw the greatest legends of tennis Andre Agassi (former world no 1) and Pete Sampras (former world no 1) practicing against each other. It was a hot summer in Canada, so Andre Agassi removed his shirt and was practicing against Pete Sampras. What a multimillion dollar moment!

Can you imagine The Celebrity Guru is witnessing a celebrity moment with the best the world has ever produced, tennis celebrities Andre Agassi & Pete Sampras? Thank you, God, for letting me witness this celebrity moment.

One day I went to watch Rogers Cup with one of my best friends, Bhavesh. I saw Indian tennis celebrity Sania Mirza (World no 1 doubles in 2015). I met her husband Pakistani Cricketer Shoaib Malik too. Just imagine my celebrity moment! The Celebrity Guru, DR. PPP, born in India, just saw playing live the No 1 Tennis female player Sania Mirza, who was born in India and representing India in Toronto from only several meters away! I could not resist, but had to cheer Sania Mirza. Generally, tennis is the silent game to watch, but I was cheering so loudly. I was saying, "Go Sania Go. Go Sania Go. Go Sania Go." Sometimes I was cheering so much that Sania Mirza would look at me during her play. In the middle of the play, she decided to go to the washroom, so she was going from the tennis grounds to the portable washroom with the security guards. I was just beside Sania Mirza. After she came from the washroom, the security officers escorted me and my friend Bhavesh out by calling some more security officers warned me not to attend the whole Rogers Cup that year. During the escort, I felt like I was on top of the world, because I proved that I am Sania Mirza's biggest tennis fan. Can you believe she was winning as long as I was watching and cheering Sania Mirza live? When I reached my friend Bhavesh's home, we learned that Sania Mirza lost. That day I learned a lot about the importance of having your fan in your life. Celebrities are nothing without their fans. Let me take this opportunity to heartily thank you for being my celebrity fans through this amazing book "You are the Celebrity". Go to youarethecelebritybook.com, as well as facebook.com/youarethecelebrity, to make our bond closer and to get your bonuses.

Several years ago, one of my brothers-in-law, Nileshkumar, gave me a tennis racket as my birthday gift. I played with it for several years until I lost it. I was heartbroken when I lost it, because there was so much sentiment attached to that racket. It was a gift from one of my best relatives. I used to play against him a lot in the USA for several hours at a time. That racket was made up of Tungsten, so it was very light. That racket was from company name "PRINCE". I felt I was the prince while playing with it. The threads were a green colour, which is eye catching and a unique colour for a tennis racket. I love to be a standout and unique. I always make sure to standout, so I can sail from the sea of sameness to the island of individuality. After that tennis racket, I bought several tennis rackets, but none of them come close to my first tennis racket.

I played lots of tennis with my best friend Bhavesh. He was a beginner when we started, but after several months, he became tennis pro. Bhavesh and I used to play for several hours in a day at several tennis grounds in Toronto. Sometimes we visited about 4 grounds, just to find a vacancy. We played in the dark too, because at 11 pm at night the tennis ground lights turned off automatically. Bhavesh and I became masters at playing without the ground lights. Can you imagine playing tennis without ground lights? Have you ever eaten in the dark? Where did your food go? If your food goes in your mouth, even in the darkness, that means you have the mastery. Same thing with playing tennis at night. Bhavesh and I played during rain too. Can you imagine playing tennis in the rain? How much heavier the ball becomes? How much more confident I was about my health?

While playing tennis, I love to count points. I love to serve. I love to play an aggressive game. I am a pro in forwards. I love to do my first serve very fast. My favourite shot in tennis is when my opponent's ball comes so high that I just play directly without letting it hit the ground.

One day, Bhavesh and I were playing as usual. The game was getting interesting. Bhavesh played his ball and I let the ball go because it was just outside of the line, but close to the line. I was 100% confident. Bhavesh thought the ball was in and he got the point. I said to Bhavesh that I am telling you because the ball was so close but it was outside of the line. I was confident because I was about one or two feet away, while he was much further away in comparison. After that huge argument, Bhavesh never played with points. We just practiced, but I never had the fun I used to getting.

I played tennis with my brother, Maheshbhai and Prakashbhai's brother in law, one of my best friends, Ronak. I took lots of trips from Toronto to the crossing lots of the states of the USA with my brother Maheshbbhai, as well as Ronak. They always let me drive their cars. I am thankful for that. Those trips helped us a lot to have family personal time for hours and hours. I survived several life-threatening moments during those driving trips. I am always grateful to God for that, as he became my savior several times. I could write whole book about those moments God saved me. Those moments made me more and more spiritual.

Finally, I retired from playing tennis. I miss playing tennis, but I saved so much time by retiring from playing. I learned a lot from tennis. When anything becomes an addiction, generally its not good, even playing tennis for non-professional tennis players.

While playing any game, I always play to win. It doesn't matter even if I play with my son or my nieces Prachi, Vidhi, Leena, and Reena or nephews Prayag, Dhairya, Dhaval and Nick, my friends or my school principals or with my father, who is my first mentor.

One day my online mentor, Murali Murthy, invited me to play tennis on his home ground. I beat him with huge win and after that day he never played tennis with me again. Are you playing to win or are you playing not to lose? That determines the result of any game. The mindset of the player who is playing to win has always more confidence than the mindset of the player who is playing not to lose. The player who is playing to win is more confident, less fearful, and more prepared than the player who is playing not to lose. I highly encourage you to approach any game or your life with the mindset of the player who is playing to win. I am happy to share this secret of success because I need you to be successful. I would love to hear from you that my book changed your life. That I changed your life.

Now you've enjoyed my two favourite games, cricket as well as tennis and the celebrity moments with cricket celebrities and tennis celebrities, you are ready to go to the final chapter of my book "You are the Celebrity".

Feel free to visit www.youarethecelebritybook.com, as well as facebook.com/youarethecelebrity, to get your bonuses and make our bond stronger.

CHAPTER 10
CELEBRITY ENTREPRENEURS

OPRAH WINFREY

O PRAH IS AN American media proprietor, talk show host, actress, producer and philanthropist. Oprah is best known for her talk show, The Oprah Winfrey Show, which has aired for 25 years nonstop.

Oprah is one of the celebrity entrepreneurs who changed millions of lives. Oprah was sexually abused multiple times by her own relatives. Oprah delivered a baby at age 14 because of sexual abuse, but that baby died within weeks. At that moment, Oprah's father told her that this is your second chance. This is your opportunity to seize this moment and make something of your life. Oprah is not only an icon for black women or women, but she is an icon of humanity. I can write a lot about Oprah, but better you google her instead. Oprah is the media mogul who now has her OWN Channel, Oprah Winfrey Network. I used to watch The Oprah Winfrey Show and learned a lot of life lessons.

In April 2012, Oprah came to Toronto to do an Oprah life class show. I went to the venue near the CN TOWER, Metro

Toronto Convention Center. I saw a line of people about 2 kilometers long, those who had already bought a ticket to the show. That show was a sold-out show. I was optimistic about seeing Oprah though. Finally, I bought my ticket from a person who was selling the tickets at almost double the price. When I entered the hall, I saw more than 5,000 people. When Oprah arrived in her green dress, she looked like a diva. I had tears of joy, because I could see her in person. One of my wildest dreams to see Oprah was fulfilled. That episode was broadcasted live world wide. People were sending responses through social media. In other countries, people were asking question via satellite. The theme was about forgiveness.

Tony Robbins and DR. Deepak Chopra were also guests on that show. I was able to see them for the first time too.

TONY ROBBINS

Tony Robbins is an author, actor, professional speaker, and philanthropist. I saw him for the first time in April 2012, when he came to Toronto with Oprah. Tony Robbins is full of energy. He walks several miles during his speeches. He has his production team with him all the time. He was raised in a poor family and became multimillionaire by inspiring people all over the world. I even saw his advertisement on the back of one of the buses when I was vacationing in Australia. I highly encourage you to watch his movie, "I am not your guru". I never saw a speaker with this kind of energy in my life. I highly encourage you to watch him live.

I watched him a second time when he came to Toronto again. This time he was the keynote speaker. Les Brown was another speaker during the same event.

BILL BRITT

Bill Britt is the father of networking. Under him are over a million networkers. Bill served in the American army. He used to be the city manager in North Carolina. In 1969, he joined one of the oldest network marketing companies, which still exists. He was driving his car from North Carolina to see the business plan of that network company by his mentor Dexter Yeager in New York. He was about to go back to his home, but he decides to meet Dexter and rest is history. He became so successful through that network marketing company that he became a multibillionaire. Though he has since passed away, rest in peace, daily he is still making several millions as the royalties of his BWW educational company help entrepreneurs all over the world. This is the power of the man with a vision.

I saw Bill Britt for the first time around late 1999 in Toronto. The person brought me to see him told me that he has his own private plane. I was surprised to see him in person because even though he was a multimillionaire, he talked about farmers and the principle of sewing and reaping. I highly encourage you to read the book, "IRON MAN SILKEN HEART: BILL BRITT'S FATHER POWER" to know more about Bill Britt. It was written by the Kumar Shivram, who became a multimillionaire because of the BWW system.

After several years, I joined same company. I enjoyed the BWW system. I never ever saw such a powerful system for any network marketing company in my life. BWW TV has several hundred success stories of people who became successful by using the BWW system and making more than a dent in the world. I've attended several functions in Canada, as well as in the USA, through the BWW system. The BWW system helps me a lot in my life. I always listen BWW CDs while driving home daily.

The basic concept of network marketing company is same. It is a win-win situation for the company and the entrepreneur, as well as the person who introduced the opportunity to the new person.

The 1% effort of 100 people is better than the 100% effort of one person. Most of the networking companies offer free mentorship.

Wow! You did it. You are the finisher. You are the Celebrity. Let's bring our relationship next level by youarethecelebritybook. com as well as facebook.com/youarethecelebrity.